"BROWNE'S INCLUSIVE GUIDELINES WILL ENCOURAGE YOU TO PICK UP YOUR PEN AND EXPRESS YOURSELF IN WAYS THAT MESSAGES DELIVERED VIA TELEPHONE OR EMAIL SIMPLY CAN'T CONVEY."

—Dorothea Johnson, author, etiquette expert, and founder of
The Protocol School of Washington®

"WHEN SAYING THANKS, THE FIRST STEP IS TO GET THE PERSON'S NAME ABSOLUTELY PERFECT. MR. OR DR.? MRS., MS., MISS, OR MX.? A UNIQUE SPELLING OF THE NAME? WHEN WE ARE CORRECTLY ADDRESSED, WE FEEL RECOGNIZED. KELLY BROWNE'S BOOK WILL GUIDE YOU TO PERFECT EXPRESSIONS OF GRATITUDE—AND HAPPY RECIPIENTS."

—Robert Hickey, author of
Honor & Respect: The Official Guide to Names, Titles, & Forms of Address

"*101 WAYS TO SAY THANK YOU* PROVIDES THE TOOLS EVERYONE *MUST* KNOW TO ELEVATE THEIR PERSONAL EXPRESSION OF GRATITUDE, WHERE ACKNOWLEDGMENTS OF KINDNESS, COMPASSION, AND RESPECT ARE KEY. KELLY MAKES IT EASIER THAN EVER TO SHOW APPRECIATION TO BUILD—AND KEEP—RELATIONSHIPS."

—Pamela Eyring, president and owner of The Protocol School of Washington®

"*101 WAYS TO SAY THANK YOU* TRANSFORMS THE CLASSIC THANK-YOU NOTE TO A LEVEL OF UNPARALLELED CLASS AND PERSONAL STYLE. HARNESS THE POWER OF GRATITUDE IN YOUR LIFE BY WRITING THE ULTIMATE THANK-YOU—IT'S THE SECRET WEAPON TO YOUR SUCCESS!"

—Debra Lassiter and April McLean, "The Etiquette Girls," of
Perfectly Polished: The Etiquette School and the Etiquette & Leadership Institute

DEDICATION

For my mother and father, Peggy and Richard Learman...
Whose gracious hearts have illuminated the world and
changed lives in ways only the stars can see.
With all my love, always...

Adams Media
An Imprint of Simon & Schuster, Inc.
100 Technology Center Drive
Stoughton, Massachusetts 02072

First Adams Media hardcover edition January 2022

ADAMS MEDIA and colophon are trademarks of Simon & Schuster.

For information about special discounts for bulk purchases, please contact Simon & Schuster Special Sales at 1-866-506-1949 or business@simonandschuster.com.

The Simon & Schuster Speakers Bureau can bring authors to your live event. For more information or to book an event contact the Simon & Schuster Speakers Bureau at 1-866-248-3049 or visit our website at www.simonspeakers.com.

Interior design by Sylvia McArdle
Illustrations and hand lettering by Priscilla Yuen

Manufactured in the United States of America

1 2022

Library of Congress Cataloging-in-Publication Data has been applied for.

ISBN 978-1-5072-1801-3
ISBN 978-1-5072-1802-0 (ebook)

Contains material adapted from the following title published by Sterling Publishing Co., Inc: *101 Ways to Say Thank You* by Kelly Browne, copyright © 2015, ISBN 978-1-4549-1560-7.

101 WAYS
TO SAY
ThankYou

NOTES *of* GRATITUDE *for* EVERY OCCASION

— KELLY BROWNE —

ADAMS MEDIA

NEW YORK LONDON TORONTO SYDNEY NEW DELHI

CONTENTS

CHAPTER 1

Thank-You NOTES 101

CHAPTER 2

Netiquette 101

CHAPTER 3

SOIRÉES and SOCIAL *Gatherings*

ACKNOWLEDGMENTS

My deepest gratitude to everyone who has embraced this book for so many years. Linda Konner, thank you! You made *all* of this possible, many times over, and I am so grateful to you always. To the entire team at Adams Media, especially Cate Prato, Leah D'Sa, Sylvia McArdle, Priscilla Yuen, and Laura Daly—I am honored; thank you *so* much! This has been an incredible journey for me, and I am so utterly grateful to you all for helping me send love, compassion, and appreciation into the world.

Everyone at Crane & Co.—thank you for your continued endorsement! Dorothea Johnson, I am forever grateful to you for always supporting me. I appreciate and adore you. Robert Hickey, your guidance on proper forms of "honor and respect" is an outstanding model of kindness for all of us—thank you for immediately stepping in to offer your valuable direction. Pamela Eyring, my deepest thanks to you and the entire Protocol School of Washington®. I applaud your work in the global community to create cultures of civility. Debra Lassiter and April McLean of Perfectly Polished: The Etiquette School—your work with our young adults has changed lives, spreading gratitude and goodwill—thank you! Motion Picture & Television Fund—to every single person who touched our lives and helped us through an excruciating time.

Thanks to all of my friends for their love, especially Sue Kovacs, Monica Salz, and Warren and Kimberly Wileman. My family—Aric, Jack, Mick, Edward, William, and Gretchen Learman Burrier; and the Mullens, Kerrigan, Gardner, and Fish families— my love always.

My father, Richard Learman—I love you and thank you endlessly for all of your valuable notes and thoughtful revisions on this book! I could not have done this without you. Greta and Ava, my gorgeous little treasures, you are my whole life. And finally, to all the angels in heaven and on earth, especially my mom—who appeared, listened, loved, and supported me when I needed it most—*thank you* from the bottom of my heart. XO

FOREWORD

Hail the handwritten note! It has been around for hundreds of years, and we will not witness its demise simply because some of its everyday functions have been replaced by digital forms of connecting. Of course, it's a given that email, texting, and telephones are most efficient for staying in touch and handling daily communications, but when it comes to a cut above, paper and pen rule.

In this updated edition, embracing the digital and diverse world we live in, Kelly Browne takes a modern, commonsense albeit elegant approach to note writing. Though highly practical, this book's lively text makes it a joy to peruse. Ms. Browne's inclusive guidelines will encourage you to pick up your pen and express yourself in ways that messages delivered via telephone or email simply can't convey. If the people of the world become a little more thoughtful about showing gratitude by writing notes, it will be in no small measure thanks to the efforts of Kelly Browne.

—Dorothea Johnson, author, etiquette expert, and founder of
The Protocol School of Washington®

How a note begins can have a huge impact on how the note is received—and even have an impact on the entire relationship. When saying thanks, the first step is to get the person's name absolutely perfect. Mr. or Dr.? Mrs., Ms., Miss, or Mx.? A unique spelling of the name? When we are correctly addressed, we feel recognized. Getting the name right may sound obvious, but it is amazing how often such a simple thing is mangled. On a note of thanks, get the name wrong and the subsequent note is diminished. Get the name right, all is well, and your gratitude is amplified.

—Robert Hickey, author of *Honor & Respect:
The Official Guide to Names, Titles, & Forms of Address*

INTRODUCTION

$\mathcal{T}hank\ you.$

These two little words may seem so simple, yet they are an incredibly power-ful way to represent gratitude and love. They can convey heartfelt meaning and create a bit of magic by flooding the recipient with warm feelings. Cultivating a spirit of gratitude in your life is so important—counting your blessings can help you remember to appreciate all that you have and will create abundance.

Are you saying thank you often enough? Remembering the thoughtfulness of our friends, loved ones, healthcare workers, or business associates with a formal note of thanks can benefit both parties when appreciation is given and received. We can feel the connection that one tiny sheet of paper can create, and it means the world to us to be acknowledged. A handwritten note on lovely paper is a classic option, but there are ways to offer your thanks online and make the sentiment just as mean-ingful and eloquent. Nothing stands out more or lets people know how much you appreciate their act of kindness than the classically personal thank-you note.

101 Ways to Say Thank You is here to help you learn how to share your appreciation through thoughtful correspondence. In this book, you'll find my personal guide to the basics in Chapter 1: Thank-You Notes 101, as well as more than one hundred sample thank-you note templates and guidance for all occasions, including romance, dinners, birthdays, weddings, babies, business, career, sympathy, the holidays, and so much more. These sample notes can provide inspiration for your own personalized messages. You'll also find a variety of quick tips for sending notes, easy checklists, online registry ideas, and even digital stationery guidance to help you say thank you with style and grace. Also included is valuable information for modern times, such as using gender-neutral pronouns and hashtagging people or companies in online thank-yous.

Studies have proven that saying thank you actually creates a chain reaction of kindness that propels a cycle of gratitude that is carried forward. No wonder many spiritual traditions, philosophers, and great thinkers value gratitude to enhance our well-being for happier, healthier lives. Imagine the positive global effect we could each have if we made showing our appreciation a part of our daily practice. Gratitude truly is the unseen silver thread that connects us all. Whether you write, post, share, tweet, or livestream your gratitude, your positive comments have the ability to brighten someone's day. Remember the magic words: *Thank you*!

CHAPTER 1

Thank-You NOTES 101

GETTING BACK TO BASICS

> *ETIQUETTE* IS A FRENCH WORD WHICH MEANS 'TICKET' OR 'LABEL.'
> DURING THE REIGN OF LOUIS XIV, THE FUNCTIONS AT THE FRENCH COURT
> WERE SO ELABORATE THAT IT BECAME NECESSARY TO GIVE EVERY VISITOR
> A TICKET (*UNE ÉTIQUETTE*) ON WHICH WERE LISTED THE FORMALITIES
> HE WAS EXPECTED TO OBSERVE. THUS, HIS BEHAVIOR, IF CORRECT, WAS
> 'ACCORDING TO THE TICKET.' IT IS IN THIS SENSE THAT WE HAVE TAKEN
> THE WORK INTO ENGLISH AND IT HAS COME TO MEAN A CODE OF CONDUCT
> OR BEHAVIOR THAT IS CONSIDERED SOCIALLY CORRECT.

— Eleanor Roosevelt, American author and first lady,
Eleanor Roosevelt's Book of Common Sense Etiquette

Just as you are dashing out the door, something catches your eye, stopping you. In the corner of the room sits the open box with the beautiful sweater Aunt Greta sent you weeks ago. Of course, you meant to thank her; it was so incredibly thoughtful of her to think of you, but somehow you just haven't done it yet. Yes, you've been so busy, but isn't that the way life is?

If you don't do it now, chances are you might forget about it later, and the last thing you want is for anyone to think you are ungrateful by not thanking them for the gift they gave you. But where do you start? What stationery should you use? What pen? What do you say? Just think for a minute before you write; it's just a few sentences.

January 16, 20__

Dear Aunt Greta,

Thanks for the sweater. I like it and hope you are well.

Love,
Ava

Close your eyes and feel the magic you felt the moment you opened the gift and write your thank-you note directly from your heart. One more time...

January 16, 20__

Dear Aunt Greta,

Thank you so much for the gorgeous cashmere sweater. It's so perfect on me and I just love it. You always find such fabulous treasures! Thank you for always making me feel so special.

Love,
Ava

The second version is much better in terms of sentiment, and, even more important, when Aunt Greta opens her mailbox and reads your thank-you note, she will feel the magic sparkle of gratitude return to her for her generosity to you. In this chapter, you will find all the information you need to write the classic handwritten thank-you note—including choosing the right stationery for the occasion, selecting a pen, learning the structure of how to write your note, and embracing energetic adjectives. Thank-You Notes 101: Getting Back to Basics will even guide you through respectful honorifics and writing the proper address to send your envelope via postal mail.

EVERYDAY STATIONERY FOR THE PERFECT THANK-YOU NOTE

The most *formal* of social stationery is the traditional fold-over note, called the "informal," and this is often used for thank-you notes following a formal event. (See the following section "An Exquisite Option: The Stationery Wardrobe" for more information.) For expressing your gratitude for everyday occasions, there are many options to choose from. Here are a few ideas:

- **Eco-friendly cards:** Recycled paper is always a great option, as is botanical "seed" paper card stock that can be planted by the recipient to grow into wild-flowers, vegetables, and herbs. Seed paper is available for all your stationery needs, including cards, envelopes, invitations, and tags.
- **Boxed fold-over notes:** Notes with "Thank You" or a small design printed on the cover of the flap are readily available at most large stores. The inside is usually blank for your note.
- **Single and boxed cards with blank interior:** Single and boxed cards with beautiful paintings, flowers, animals, photographs, or quotes on the front that are blank on the inside are perfect for expressing your sentiment and allowing your personality to shine through.
- **Thank-you cards with interior inscription:** Sometimes these cards give you just the right words when you can't find your own. Always add a personal note along with your name.
- **Blank card stock:** Available in all colors and weights with matching envelopes, these are not only affordable and easy to have on hand; they also provide wonderful ways to create your own designs.
- **Handcrafted stationery:** If you really want to make your mark, handcrafted stationery is perfectly personal. Whether you choose to design your own or order from a stationery house, there are many types of papers, ribbons, and adornments. Tip: Ellen Weldon Design is a great resource to use for crafting your vision. Visit www.weldondesign.com.

AN EXQUISITE OPTION: THE STATIONERY WARDROBE

A "stationery wardrobe" consists of a selection of choices of versatile paper stationery that can be readily used for any occasion and gives you the opportunity to reflect your unique personality. From the lavishly expensive to very affordable, your choice of papers—color, size, weight, and printing—makes a statement about you and is a valuable social and business tool. Start your stationery wardrobe with the pieces that you will use most often, perhaps one for your thank-you notes and one for writing letters. Here are the main components of a typical stationery wardrobe:

- **Correspondence cards (4¼" × 6½"):** The most versatile stationery for writing short notes, thank-yous, and invitations; only the front is used. These can be printed with your monogram, crest, or name and are usually a heavier paper weight.
- **Informals (5¼" × 3½"):** While the name might be confusing, "informals" are actually *formal* notes. Folded in half and often referred to as "fold-overs," informals can be printed with your name, crest, or monogram on the front. For a level of high formality, choose paper colors like ecru or white, with your full name in black engraving.
- **Single-sheet stationery:** This type of paper is printed with your name and street address at the top. You can choose the size and weight of the paper, which will depend on the length and formality of your letters. Use a blank piece if you need a second sheet. Lighter in weight, this paper can fit through most printers, if necessary.
- **Note sheets (6⅜" × 8½"):** Perfect for social letters and correspondence.
- **Monarch or executive stationery (7¼" × 10½"):** These sheets are used for both social letters and personal business letters.
- **Standard letter sheets (8½" × 11"):** Most frequently used for business letters.
- **Envelopes:** Keep in mind that most people create stationery wardrobes so they can use one size of envelope for several different sizes of paper. Envelopes should include a return address, but including your name is optional.
- **Calling cards:** Varying in size and similar to a business card, calling cards are for new acquaintances. They include your personal contact information, such as your name, phone number, email address, and website or home address. You can simply use your name and phone number or your name and email address— it's up to you.

Printing Processes: Flat, Thermographic, Engraved, and Embossed

Personalized stationery always makes a memorable impression. There are many kinds of printing methods for every budget—here are some of the most common:

- **Flat printing:** Simply the combination of ink and paper, flat printing is the most economical method to create personalized stationery.
- **Thermography:** Thermography is a popular choice for affordability and availability of designs. To produce the raised-print effect of the design or letters on the paper, resin powder and ink are heated and dried. This results in a textured impression that can be felt.
- **Engraving:** Engraving is the most elegant and expensive way to print your stationery at the outset, but once your initials, name, or business name have been die-cast using a metal casting process, you can use the same mold again and again, making it cost-effective in the long run.
- **Embossing:** Like the engraving process, a metal plate or cast is cut to create your information. The plate is then stamped into the paper to create a "raised" effect. For a "debossing" effect, the plate is depressed into the card stock to depress or create a "lowered" effect.

WRITING INSTRUMENTS—QUILLS, INKS, AND PENS

There are endless options of writing instruments to communicate the written word. Your choices reflect your personal style and should suit the occasion. Here are a few etiquette tips to keep in mind as you decide what's best for you:

- **Formal thank-you notes:** Black or blue ink pens are always the preferred method (rather than ballpoint pens) when sending a formal thank-you note. You might choose a fountain pen, gel, rollerball, or a fancy feather quill and ink. Tip: Disposable fountain pens are affordable and make a great impression.
- **Casual thank-you notes:** Whatever pen speaks to you is the pen you should use to express your heartfelt words of appreciation. From chocolate-brown ink on crisp pink paper to dazzling silver on jet-black card stock to holiday colors of the season, the pen that you feel good about using is always the "write" choice!

HANDWRITTEN VERSUS PRINTING A NOTE FROM YOUR COMPUTER

Traditionally, thank-you notes are handwritten neatly on good-quality stationery, are free of spelling errors or crossed-out words, and are written in blue or black ink. They are personal, gracious, and thoughtful. In today's tech-savvy world, the handwritten note is even more treasured. However, many of us feel embarrassed by our handwriting, which can make writing a thank-you note a very intimidating and awkward situation—especially when we want to come across as graceful. If this is the case, you might prefer a digital thank-you as the best way to express yourself.

So which is worse, not sending a thank-you note or typing one? The answer is obvious—*not* sending one. There is absolutely no reason you cannot create your thank-you notes on your computer or mobile device. In fact, there are several advantages if you choose to go the computer-generated route:

- You can use the grammar and spell-check function in your word-processing program and catch errors you may have otherwise missed.
- Your note will be neat and legible. Consider using a basic script font that looks like handwriting, but stay away from the styles that are ornate and difficult to read.
- You can better plan out your words because you can delete what you wrote and start over! We are often committed to what we have started in handwritten notes because we don't want to waste the paper or write it all over again.

It's very easy to print different sizes of paper on your printer. Use the "page setup" menu when creating your new document and adjust the page size to that of your paper and envelope.

Make sure you do a test run on inexpensive copy paper before using your best stationery. You can find a wide variety of gorgeous paper in stores and online retailers, ranging from high quality to inexpensive. As long as it isn't too thick or too small for your printer, high-end preprinted personalized stationery will work, and will leave a lasting impression. Watermarked, 100 percent cotton paper, which is available in varying weights, always looks more elegant than copy paper.

WRITING THE CLASSIC THANK-YOU NOTE

Now that you have your pen and paper in hand, it's easy to write a thank-you note because the format is always the same: the date, your salutation, your personal thank-you message, the closing, and your signature.

You can break down the writing process into these steps:

1. Write the Date

January 16, 20 __

2. Write the Salutation or Greeting

Dear (person's name),

- "Dear" is the most popular salutation to use, but you can also use "Dearest" for a loved one or your own term of endearment, depending on the situation.
- Remember to use a comma following the salutation and addressee's name for all handwritten notes, social or casual.
- If you're writing a thank-you note to a couple, you can write the note to one of them and mention the other in the text of the note, or you can address it to both of them.
- Use the appropriate honorific ahead of the person's last name for formal notes. For example, "Dear (Mr./Mrs./Ms./Mx.) Browne." For casual or intimate relationships, it is only necessary to use the person's first name.

3. Write the Content of Your Thank-You Note

Thank the person as genuinely and graciously as you can. Try to add something extra, such as "I look forward to seeing you soon," or "I hope you're doing well," or "My mother sends her love," or even the popular "Let's grab coffee sometime!" If you are writing a thank-you note for a gift, think about the exciting moment you opened it.

4. Write the Closing

If you aren't sure what is appropriate for the situation, "Sincerely yours" is always an elegant choice and in accordance with social protocol. Here are some other suggestions for specific circumstances:

For Formal and Business Notes

- Sincerely,
- Very sincerely,
- Sincerely yours,
- Very sincerely yours,

For Thank-You Notes of Love and Friendship

- Affectionately,
- Love always,
- With affection,
- Yours truly,
- Fondly,
- Truly yours,
- Your friend,
- Love,
- Warmly,
- Yours,

For Thank-You Notes for Special Gifts and Favors

- Gratefully,
- Gratefully yours,

For Thank-You Notes to Clergy and Government Officials

- Faithfully yours,
- Respectfully,
- Respectfully yours,
- Sincerely yours,
- Yours faithfully,

For General Thank-Yous

- Best regards,
- Best wishes for (insert sentiment),
- Best wishes,
- My best wishes for (insert sentiment),

5. Add Your Signature

This can be your first name or your first and last name.

- Most commonly, people sign their first name for personal relationships and their full name for formal or professional ones.
- Make sure your signature is legible. Often signatures become a bunch of circles or a squiggly line, and the poor recipient of your note is left baffled as to who you might be.
- If you write and print your thank-you note from your computer, it is best to handwrite your name.
- If your signature is illegible, you might want to use personalized stationery.

6. Formatting

Your note should be formatted like this on the page:

. . . .

January 16, 20 ___

Dear _____,

Thank you for the very generous gift card! I desperately needed and wished to get a new _____, and now I can finally get it, thanks to you. I am so excited and truly appreciate that you are always thinking of me. Thank you for making my wish come true!

With all my love,

_____

. . . .

> 66 GRATITUDE IS THE MOST EXQUISITE FORM OF COURTESY. 99
>
> —Jacques Maritain, French philosopher

SEVEN DOS FOR ELEGANT NOTES

1. **Do handwrite your note neatly**, without mistakes, on good-quality stationery using your favorite ink pen.
2. **Do use glowing superlatives and energetic adjectives** like *fabulous*, *amazing*, *delightful*, and *extraordinary*. Be creative. Really think about the moment you opened the gift and how you felt, and then tell the recipient about it. Be expansive and passionate to convey your emotion.
3. **Do mention in your note how you plan to use the gift.** This shows that the gift was well chosen, and that's one of the best ways to say thank you.
4. **Do add a compliment**, such as "You have wonderful taste," or "How do you always know just what to get for me?," or "You are such a thoughtful and kind person," or "I'm so grateful to have you in my life." Everybody likes to know that they are appreciated.
5. **Do keep your note to a paragraph or two at the most.** Remember, it is a note, not a letter. You can make it longer if you wish to, but it is not expected.
6. **Do make each note sound special and unique** to the person, situation, and gift. Thank-you notes should never feel generic.
7. **Do remember to write a draft.** If you have trouble organizing your thoughts, just write out your note first on scrap paper or type it up on your computer, then copy it neatly.

The *Thank-You* Thesaurus:
Glowing Superlatives and Energetic Adjectives

Try some of these words to add a little excitement to your notes!

AMAZING

ASTONISHING

ASTOUNDING

ATTRACTIVE

AWE-INSPIRING

BEAUTIFUL

BEYOND BELIEF

BRIGHT

BRILLIANT

CHARMING

COLORFUL

DAZZLING

ENCHANTING

EXCELLENT

EXCEPTIONAL

EXTRAORDINARY

FABULOUS

FINE-LOOKING

GENEROUS

GLEAMING

GLISTENING

GLOWING

GOOD-LOOKING

GORGEOUS

HANDSOME

HARD TO BELIEVE

INCANDESCENT

INCONCEIVABLE

INCREDIBLE

IRIDESCENT

LIVELY

LUCKY

LOVELY

LUMINOUS

MARVELOUS

MIRACULOUS

MULTICOLORED

OBSESSED

OUT OF THIS WORLD

OUTSTANDING

RADIANT

REMARKABLE

RICH

SHIMMERING

SHINING

SPARKLING

SPECTACULAR

SPLENDID

STARTLING

STRIKING

STUNNING

SURPRISING

UNBELIEVABLE

VIBRANT

VIVID

WHIMSICAL

WONDERFUL

AND THE ENVELOPE, PLEASE...

The envelope is an important part of your thank-you note's package, so please don't cast it off as insignificant. Remember, it's the very first thing the recipient experiences when your note of appreciation arrives, and you want to make a favorable impression immediately.

Labeling Your Envelope

- **Formal envelopes:** Only the addressee's name and address should be on the front of the envelope with the state name written out, not abbreviated. The return address should be written on the back flap of the envelope, *without* the return addressee's name.
- **Casual and business envelopes:** It's always best to use the appropriate honorific ahead of the addressee's name, if possible, especially for business communication. (You'll learn more about honorifics in the next section.) The addressee's name should begin at the center of the envelope with the street address directly underneath it. The next line is the city, state, and zip code.
- **Your return address:** The return address may be written or preprinted on the back flap, as in the formal protocol, or on the top left corner of the envelope, with the return addressee's name. Here you may choose to include your honorific ahead of your full name, if you wish.

How It Should Look

The front of your casual and business envelopes should look like this:

Your Name
1234 Street Avenue
Town, ST 90000-1234

Mrs. Gift Giver
4321 Street Avenue
Anytown, ST 80000-4321

Insert your thank-you note into the envelope with the folded side up and the front of the note facing toward you so the flap of the envelope closes down over the front of the note.

Simple Dos and Don'ts for the Elegant Envelope

- **Do make sure you double-check the address** before you write it on the front of the envelope.
- **Do handwrite your envelope if your note is handwritten** (which is always best). Don't send a typed or computer-printed thank-you note with a hand-addressed envelope. Whatever you choose, they should match.
- **Do use the "tool" tab, then "envelope" setting in your word-processing program** to set up your return address and delivery address information. Print your envelope from your printer using the font, text color, and text size of your choice.
- **Do consider elevating the envelope experience by using an "envelope seal."** This can be wax, gold foil, a monogrammed sticker, or even an elegant sticker with your business logo.

- **Don't use "stick-on" return address labels from promotional companies** if you can avoid it, as they look impersonal. You can easily design your own labels and return address self-inking stampers at online stationery houses that make a lasting impression and are also a wonderful gift.
- **Do include the last four digits of the nine-digit zip code** for US addresses—for example, 91000-1234. Your mail will get to its destination faster! If you don't know the full zip code, check it online at www.usps.com.
- **Do check out the variety of stamps** and personalized stamped envelopes available at your local post office or online. Whether you are celebrating holidays, honoring diversity, championing causes close to your heart, or paying tribute to global achievements, one little detail of a stamp can send a bit of mindful awareness into the world while enhancing your presentation. Think of the impact you can make!

USING HONORIFICS AND RESPECTFUL FORMS OF ADDRESS

An honorific is any title that shows respect or honor, such as the Hon., the Rev., Dr., Mr., Mrs., Miss, Ms., and the gender-neutral honorifics Mx. (often pronounced "mix") and "Mixter." Ask someone what honorific they would like you to use or to be identified by if they have not made their preference known. Include the appropriate honorific in the formal and business thank-you note as well as on the envelope. However, if you are unsure of which honorific to use, on very *informal* casual notes, it is acceptable not to include one. Here are some tips for addressing envelopes using honorifics:

- **For yourself:** Avoid using an honorific with your own name when signing a thank-you note.
- **Official titles:** Always check the appropriate title when addressing your note to a government official, an academic, a military officer, or a member of the clergy or royalty. Here their rank or official title must be used.
- **Man over age sixteen:** Use "Mr.," short for "Mister," regardless of their marital status.

- **Young lady under age thirteen:** Use "Miss" in a formal or social note and if you are addressing an older woman if you know it is her preference.
- **Professional woman:** Use "Ms." even if she is married. Use for divorced women reverting to their maiden name or when you are uncertain of a woman's marital status.
- **Married woman:** Use "Mrs." when addressing a married woman who is using her first name, her maiden name, and her husband's surname:

    Mrs. Her First Name + Her Maiden Name + Husband's Surname

- **Married woman—formal:** Use "Mrs." when *formally* addressing a married woman who has adopted her husband's surname, followed by her husband's full name:

    Mrs. His First Name + His Middle Name + His Surname

- **Divorced woman:** Some divorced women reverting to their maiden names will use *Ms. + First Name + Maiden Name*. Use "Mrs." for a divorced woman retaining her married name, followed by her first, maiden, and married names:

    Mrs. Her First Name + Her Maiden Name + Husband's Surname

- **Widow:** Address a widow as "Mrs. *Husband's Surname*" if it is her preference.

- **Married opposite-sex couple—formal:** Use "Mr. and Mrs." for formal notes when addressing a married opposite-sex couple with the same last name, followed by the husband's name, so it includes the first, middle, and last names:

    Mr. and Mrs. His First Name + His Middle Name + His Surname

    However, some couples prefer to include both of their first, or given, names:

    Mr. and Mrs. His First Name + Her First Name + His Surname

- **Same-sex couple:** According to etiquette expert Robert Hickey, "When addressing an envelope to a same-sex couple, where each member uses different surnames, list each name fully—in alphabetical order." This is also a formula you can use for any couple of equal precedence who use different surnames. For example:

Mr. Thomas Appleton and Mr. Richard Zappa

If both partners use the same surname, list them in alphabetical order by the first name, like this:

Ms. Adeline Henderson and Ms. Zelda Henderson

- **Couple with one person of higher rank—formal:** The name of the higher-ranking person is listed first when addressing formal correspondence. For example, address a doctor and their partner using the same surname, as follows:

Dr. and (Mrs./Mr./Ms./Mx.) First Name + Middle Name + Surname

If the doctor and their partner are using *different* last names, then, because the earned title of "doctor" is of a higher rank, the doctor's name should appear on the line above the partner, like this:

Dr. First Name + Middle Name + Surname
(Mrs./Mr./Ms./Mx.) First Name + Middle Name + Surname

Or, both full names may appear on the same line, like this:

Dr. First Name + Middle Name + Surname and
(Mrs./Mr./Ms./Mx.) First Name + Middle Name + Surname

Easy Etiquette

To learn more about honorifics, read Robert Hickey's *Honor & Respect: The Official Guide to Names, Titles, & Forms of Address.* Mr. Hickey's classic book is an essential resource and reference addition to your library for timeless guidelines on proper forms of address. For more information, visit: www.psow.edu.

SENDING YOUR GLOBAL GRATITUDE—INTERNATIONAL FORMS OF ADDRESS

Always be sure to verify international addresses and ensure that they follow the formatting guidelines and conventions of the countries where you are sending your mail.

Formatting the Envelope

According to the US Postal Service, all mail should include:

- The return address—which is the address of the sender—in the upper left-hand corner, and
- The recipient's name and delivery address written to the right and center of the envelope.

Both should be printed on the same side of the envelope or package using uppercase Roman letters and numbers: ABC, 123. In some countries the format may vary, but the standard order of the international delivery address should be addressed this way:

Line 1: Name of addressee. Example: *Honorific + Recipient Name*
Line 2: Street address or post office box number. Example: *1234 Street Drive*
Line 3: City or town name, other principal subdivision (such as province, state, or county), and postal code (if known). Example: *London W1P 6HQ*
Line 4: Full country name. Example: *England*

Specific Country Examples

Here are a few examples for sending international correspondence:

Australia: https://auspost.com.au
Recipient's Name
House Number + Street Name
Suburb and State/Territory
Postcode
Australia

Canada: www.canadapost.ca
Recipient's Name
House Number + Street Name
City, Province, Postal Code
Canada

China: http://english.chinapost.com.cn
Recipient's Name
House Number + Street Name, City
Postal Code + Province
People's Republic of China

France: www.laposte.fr
Recipient's Name
House Number + Street Name
Postal Code, Town Name
France

India: www.indiapost.gov.in
Recipient's Name
House Number + Name of House/Building
Street/Road Name
Locality
Post Office Name + PIN Code
POST TOWN/CITY (written in BLOCK letters)
India

Ireland: www.anpost.com
Recipient's Name
House Number + Street Name
Name of County
Eircode/Postal Code
Ireland

Mexico: www.gob.mx/correosdemexico
Recipient's Name
Street Type + Street Name + House Number
Neighborhood, Municipality
Postal Code, City, State
Mexico

Italy: https://poste.it
Recipient's Name
Street Name + House Number
Postal Code, City, Province Code
Italy

United Kingdom: www.royalmail.com
Recipient's Name
House Number + Street Name
City/Town Name, Postal Code
(Country: England/Northern Ireland/
Scotland/Wales)
United Kingdom

United Emirates: www.epg.gov.ae
Recipient's Name
Title and/or Company Name
PO Box
Emirate
UAE

> ❝ WHEN OUR COMMUNITY IS IN A STATE OF PEACE, IT CAN SHARE
> THAT PEACE WITH NEIGHBORING COMMUNITIES, AND SO ON. WHEN
> WE FEEL LOVE AND KINDNESS TOWARDS OTHERS, IT NOT ONLY MAKES
> OTHERS FEEL LOVED AND CARED FOR, BUT IT HELPS US
> ALSO TO DEVELOP INNER HAPPINESS AND PEACE. ❞
>
> —Dalai Lama, Tibetan spiritual leader

THE GOLDEN RULES FOR TIMELY THANK-YOU SUCCESS

It's easy to let time accidentally pass after an event or following the receipt of a gift. Here are some ways to remind yourself to send a thank-you note:

* Send your thank-you note immediately; then you won't forget. If you need extra time, that's all right, but be sure to send a thank-you note within two weeks of the event or receiving a gift.
* Keep the gift, enclosure card, or packing slip in sight as a reminder to write the note.
* Add a thank-you reminder to your digital device, paper calendar, or to-do list.
* Keep in mind that a phone call never counts as a thank-you! A note must be sent after the call.

Damage Control for Late Thank-You Notes

At some point, you will likely be faced with having to send a late thank-you note. Regardless of the tardiness, it is still imperative to send one. Yes, the person may be hurt or offended that you did not show your gratitude in a timely manner, but it will be appreciated nonetheless and is important. Here are some points to consider:

* **How late are you?**—If you are within days or a week or two of the reasonable two-week time frame, simply send your note. If, however, you are sending a thank-you note for a gift you received seven months earlier—be honest. You can

always simply convey your moment of realization and your apologies, and then continue with your note. For example, "While filling the gorgeous vase you gave me for our wedding with beautiful red roses, it suddenly occurred to me that I never sent you a thank-you note! Please accept my gracious apologies. We love it and will treasure it always."

* **Just immediately say thank you!**—You can always personally connect to the gift-giver to acknowledge the gift straightaway and then follow it up with a handwritten note. Sometimes the extra touch of personal contact can help smooth a situation over, especially if you share a sweet moment; for example, describing something funny that happened on your honeymoon or how you felt when you heard your baby cry for the first time.

* **Heard it through the grapevine**—The worst scenario is when you hear from someone else that the person who gave you the gift is quite upset that you never thanked them! Often, we are so swept up in life that we occasionally do just simply *forget*—or, your thank-you note could have gotten lost in the mail. Nevertheless, rather than risk a ruined relationship, just expressing the truth will usually appease the person who is upset. For example, "I am very sorry and no excuse will be enough. I truly appreciated your kindness and generosity..." If the gift-giver chooses to discontinue a relationship because you weren't grateful enough—so be it. At least you did express your gratitude. Just embrace it as a life lesson on how important expressing your appreciation is.

> AN INVITATION OR THANK-YOU NOTE ISN'T A DUTY OR FORMALITY—
> IT'S AN AUTHENTIC EXPRESSION OF INCLUSIVITY. A TICKET THAT
> WELCOMES RECIPIENTS INTO YOUR LIFE, WHERE THEY WILL FEEL
> ACKNOWLEDGED, APPRECIATED, AND SIGNIFICANT.
>
> —Crane & Co., *The Spirit of Modern Etiquette*

EVEN THOUGH IT'S LATE, THANK YOU!—SAMPLE NOTES

Here are sample notes you can use for inspiration. Modify or copy them when you have to send a late thank-you note.

BELATED THANK YOU FOR THE GIFT

Dear _____,

I should have written this to you ages ago—please forgive my delay! I want you to know how sincerely grateful I am to you for your thoughtfulness. In fact, every time (I see it/use it/remember the moment) I think of you and am reminded how truly blessed I am to have you in my life. Thank you for thinking of me always.

Sincerely yours,

_____

. . . .

Dear _____,

I have no excuse! Regardless of my tardiness, I absolutely loved the (name of gift) you sent me. Now that I have it, I don't know how I ever survived without it. Thank you so very much for taking the time to find me the perfect gift.

With my appreciation,

_____

CHAPTER 2

Netiquette 101

VIRTUAL GRATITUDE

> "THERE'S LOTS OF WAYS TO BE AS A PERSON, AND SOME PEOPLE EXPRESS THEIR DEEP APPRECIATION IN DIFFERENT WAYS, BUT ONE OF THE WAYS THAT I BELIEVE PEOPLE EXPRESS THEIR APPRECIATION TO THE REST OF HUMANITY IS TO MAKE SOMETHING WONDERFUL AND PUT IT OUT THERE. AND YOU NEVER MEET THE PEOPLE, YOU NEVER SHAKE THEIR HANDS, YOU NEVER HEAR THEIR STORY OR TELL YOURS, BUT SOMEHOW, IN THE ACT OF MAKING SOMETHING WITH A GREAT DEAL OF CARE AND LOVE, SOMETHING IS TRANSMITTED THERE. AND IT'S A WAY OF EXPRESSING TO THE REST OF OUR SPECIES OUR DEEP APPRECIATION."
>
> —Steve Jobs, cofounder of Apple Computer

Were it not for the brilliant minds who imagined the possibilities of digital communication, we would not have the endless benefits of technology to enable us to connect. From business to personal communication, these digital tools are an essential part of our daily lives. Our virtual devices create the convenience for us to shop online, champion causes, close deals, and instantaneously send a gracious thank-you! As we connect to each other, it's important to respect our differences, promote gratitude, celebrate love and kindness, and embrace diversity, for we truly are citizens of the world.

In this chapter, you'll learn when you can send a digital thank-you note via email along with the best format to follow, pearls of wisdom to remember when online, and tips for creating registries and wish lists in stores and digital platforms.

WHEN IS IT ACCEPTABLE TO SEND AN EMAIL THANK-YOU NOTE?

While email is the least-preferred way to send a formal thank-you note, it is a viable alternative in more casual business and personal communications. For example, if your best friend shared their mama's secret family recipe via email, it would be perfectly acceptable to send an email thank-you. On the other hand, formality reigns when sending thank-you notes for wedding presents or baby gifts. Always use your best judgment.

If you aren't sure about sending an email thank-you note, don't. Remember, in today's tech-savvy world, handwritten notes are always greatly appreciated. Make an impact and leave a lasting personal impression.

> BE GRATEFUL FOR YOUR LIFE, EVERY DETAIL OF IT, AND YOUR FACE WILL COME TO SHINE LIKE A SUN, AND EVERYONE WHO SEES IT WILL BE MADE GLAD AND PEACEFUL. PERSIST IN GRATITUDE, AND YOU WILL SLOWLY BECOME ONE WITH THE SUN OF LOVE, AND LOVE WILL SHINE THROUGH YOU ITS ALL-HEALING JOY.
>
> —Rumi, Persian poet

PROPER EMAIL FORMATTING

Sending your email thank-you note is easy. The format differs from the ink-and-paper version. The date and time stamps are automatically included, so there is no need to write that information in the body of your note. Ideally, your email should include:

1. **Recipient's email address:** Make sure you have the correct email address of the person you are sending your note to. If that person has emailed you before, you should be able to quickly search for their contact information in your old emails and add it to your address book for future reference.

2. **Your name:** It is always a good idea to set your name in your email preferences so your recipient can quickly identify the email in their inbox. For example, if your email is *YourName@mindful.com*, you would want the recipient's inbox to show your name properly formatted with correct capitalization, like this: *Your Name—YourName@mindful.com*.

3. **CC:** If you want to "cc," or "carbon copy," another person on your email and you *want* your recipient to see whom you have copied, then insert their email address in this field. Remember that the person you have copied might click on "reply all" and respond to everyone on the email. If you want to control a group response, another option would be to forward your email to the recipient to avoid any errors.

4. **BCC:** The "blind carbon copy" field is used for security and privacy. For example, if you are sending an email blast to a group of people, use "BCC" on the occasions when you *don't* want your recipients to see the other email addresses you are including. Not only does this prevent a possible malware infection of capturing a group of emails; it also keeps bulk recipients from hitting "reply all" and responding to everyone publicly copied.

5. **Subject:** Include a few words in the subject line so the recipient knows what your email is about, and so it's easier to access email content at a later date. For example, "Thank you for lunch!"

6. **Body:** Include the following in the body of your note:
   - **Salutation:** "Dear," "Hi," "Hello," "Good (morning/afternoon/evening)," or other terms of endearment are appreciated but are not always necessary for a casual note. Follow this with the recipient's name and a comma or colon. Use your judgment and consider what is appropriate for each situation.
   - **Recipient's name:** Use the recipient's first name or, when appropriate, the correct honorific, followed by their first name or surname: "Dear Morgan" or "Dear Ms. Jones," for example. Always check to make sure you have spelled the recipient's name correctly.

- **Your note:** Your note should follow the basic spirit of "Writing the Classic Thank-You Note" as outlined in Chapter 1. Be sure to keep it brief, use proper grammar, spell-check, verify punctuation, and read it over to make sure autocorrected text is accurate. Always avoid using profanity and acronyms.
- **Emoticons and GIFs:** Emojis and GIFs inserted into your text are always fun to use. While they are perfect for casual notes or text messages, you should avoid them when you are sending a formal or business note.
- **Capital letters and exclamation points!:** Since the tone of your voice cannot be heard in an email, choose your words carefully to convey your emotion. Do remember that overusing exclamation points and CAPITAL LETTERS can be interpreted as "screaming."
- **Closing:** To signal the end of your email note, use "Sincerely," "Love," "Cheers," or whatever you feel is suitable for the occasion.
- **Signature:** Always include your name, as it is your electronic signature. Depending on the situation or recipient, use your first name, full name, or initials. Do consider setting your signature stamp in your email preferences and customizing it to include your closing, name, and, if you wish, your pronoun preference, telephone contact(s), email, business address, business logo, website address, and social media handles.
- **Attachments:** A picture or video is worth a thousand words! If you care to share, attach a visual so your recipient can feel your appreciation. When including a photo, video, or document, such as your resume or PDF file, make sure to reference it in the body of your note so the recipient knows to look for it.

Your email should look like this:

(Automatic date and time stamp)

To: Their Name—TheirName@grateful.com

CC: (insert email address or leave blank if you don't want to "copy" another recipient)

BCC: (insert email address or leave blank if you don't want to "blind carbon copy" another recipient)

From: Your Name—YourName@mindful.com

Subject: Thank You!

Dear _____,

Thank you so much for lunch today! Not only was it delicious, but it's always great to spend time with you. Next time, definitely my treat.

During lunch, I mentioned I would send you my *LinkedIn* profile: (insert link here). I would really appreciate any recommendations, leads, or thoughts you might have. Working at (insert name of company) would be my dream job. Please let me know what your schedule looks like over the next few weeks so we can set something up.

Thank you again!
Cheers,
_____ (your name)
(555) 765-4321—mobile
www.websitename.com
Link to *LinkedIn* Profile
Link to Social Media

THANKING A BUSINESS ONLINE USING SOCIAL MEDIA

Social media websites offer the ability for consumers to post meaningful ways of thanking a business for their exemplary service. These online tips, reviews, and endorsements have become a vital component in a thriving business. So the next time you've had a great experience, take a minute and let that business know! Here are some easy tips for posting your online gratitude:

- Crowdsourced business review websites, like *Yelp*, have become the go-to resource for everything from hair salons to doggie spas to restaurants. If you've encountered a business or employee who's gone above and beyond, your star ranking, review, and pictures can support that business or create an opportunity for an employee to be recognized.
- If you've had a great experience, post a comment or picture on your social media tagging the company's profile or using their hashtag. For example:

  - *#Thankyou! Jerry @LocalStore for expediting my order! Great customer service!*
  - *Thanks @LocalBakery for making the most delicious #birthdaycake ever!*
  - *This #LocalRestaurant truly makes the very #bestsushi in #yourtown! Thank you for the delicious dinner and great service!*

SOCIAL MEDIA: PEGGY'S PEARLS OF WISDOM

My mother's pearls of wisdom are timeless and will forever make a difference in promoting civility and global respect, online or off. Regardless of social media claims of privacy, nothing you post, share, like, tweet, or create online will be private, and how you represent yourself online is key to your success. Remember these adages and leave a digital impact.

- **"Think Before You Speak."**—The same rule applies when you text, email, message, or post on social media anything that might be considered hurtful. Written words don't always come across in the same spirit as they might if you were to say them in person, because your tone of voice can't be heard. Even if you are just "joking around" or "just kidding," not everyone may have your sense of humor or want to be publicly teased. You also can't unsend an email or take back a text, and even if you delete your post, picture, message, or tweet, someone may already have taken a screenshot. So THINK before you post!

- **"Mind Your Own Business!"**—Hiding behind the virtual armor of a computer screen, people have become more brazen about posting aggressive judgmental attacks against someone else's personal choices, religious beliefs, or political affiliations that are literally none of their business or yours. Rather than engage with outrageous online behavior—unfollow, unfriend, block that person, or make yourself private. Removing yourself and setting a boundary makes a statement without engaging. When people show you who they are—*believe them*.

- **"If You Wouldn't Say It in Person, Don't Say It Behind Their Back."**—Never email, text, or post on social media anything negative about someone or a compromising photo that might be harmful to that person's reputation. For one thing, it's inconsiderate and impolite. For another, the consequences of your action might cause a backlash against you if someone presses a legal issue. If someone asks you to remove something you have posted about them, do it. Likewise, if someone posts something mean-spirited about you and they have refused to remove it, take a screenshot and report it to the social media company.

Easy Etiquette

Remember, you aren't born with good manners and social graces; you must learn them.

ONLINE GIFT REGISTRIES AND THANK-YOU LISTS

From birthdays, babies, weddings, collecting charity donations, or just because, many popular sites offer online or in-store gift registry tools to help keep you organized so you never miss sending a thank-you note. The steps are usually simple and allow you to create a wish list for almost any occasion. Here are a few tips:

- Create an online account with the store, usually with a username and password.
- Create your registry or wish list for the desired occasion with the ability to send your items to a preferred address.
- As items are received, you can manage what gifts and sender notes you have received via most digital platforms, where purchased items are listed with the sender's name and contact information. Some sites will allow you to send a digital thank-you note directly to the person who sent you a gift or allow you to check off a box when you have sent your own.
- Returning a gift usually isn't a problem if you receive something you want to exchange or that was not on your registry. Some popular sites also offer free returns. Simply access the order number on the packing slip and follow the return instructions. If the packing slip is not included, hang on to the box, where tracking information is usually marked on the label.

SOIRÉES and SOCIAL
Gatherings
THANKS FOR HAVING ME

> I LOOKED AROUND AND THOUGHT ABOUT MY LIFE. I FELT GRATEFUL.
> I NOTICED EVERY DETAIL. THAT IS THE KEY TO TIME TRAVEL. YOU CAN
> ONLY MOVE IF YOU ARE ACTUALLY IN THE MOMENT. YOU HAVE TO BE
> WHERE YOU ARE TO GET WHERE YOU NEED TO GO.

—Amy Poehler, American actor

Cultivating an active social calendar is an important element in creating a successful and fulfilling life. Social events like dinner parties, charity events, art openings, and gatherings with friends and family not only keep you engaged in the rich tapestry of life; they often lead to new and exciting relationships and opportunities as well. Without the occasional soirée, gala, or reception to look forward to, when would you ever have an excuse to get dressed up?

Social events also represent cherished time together with friends and loved ones, celebrating life. So the next time you step out in style, let your hosts know what a great time you had by thanking them for inviting you. A grateful guest is a frequent guest!

In this chapter, you will find tips for writing the social thank-you note, as well as the golden rules for notes and social media success, followed by thank-you notes you can use or be inspired by to create your own.

WRITING THE SOCIAL THANK-YOU NOTE

All the same basic rules you learned in Chapter 1 apply here, too, so feel free to refer back to that chapter for a refresher. Here are some additional tips:

- The use of honorifics is still important for notes about social events. If you're sending a thank-you note to your dear friend's parents for inviting you to an event, like a wedding, you would want to be courteous by including the appropriate honorific as a sign of respect to that relationship.
- Pay attention to your closing as well. A formal honorific requires an elegant closing. "Sincerely" or "Sincerely yours" are more appropriate choices than casual closings such as "Thanks again."
- The fold-over informal note or social stationery in white or ecru is always the best choice. Black or blue ink is always the traditional choice when you write a social thank-you note.

> 66 APPRECIATION CAN CHANGE A DAY, EVEN CHANGE A LIFE.
> YOUR WILLINGNESS TO PUT IT INTO WORDS IS ALL THAT IS NECESSARY. 99
>
> —Margaret Cousins, Irish poet

THE FORMAL SOCIAL ENVELOPE

For formal thank-you notes, the socially correct envelope format is slightly different. The first option is to stagger the lines, with the recipient's name centered on the envelope; followed by the street address underneath and slightly to the right of center; followed by the city, state, and zip code underneath and slightly farther to the right of the address. There should be no abbreviations; everything should be spelled out.

The front of the formal envelope should look like this:

Honorific + First Name + Middle/Maiden Name + Surname
    1234 Street Place
        City, State 80000-4321

Or, all lines can be centered, like this:

Honorific + First Name + Middle/Maiden Name + Surname
1234 Street Place
City, State 80000-4321

The return address should be printed or handwritten in your best penmanship on the back flap of the envelope. While you can include your formal name, the preferred style is to use only your address. The back flap of the envelope should look like this:

9000 Avenue Road
City, State 10000-1234

Easy Etiquette

Consider purchasing a handheld embosser. This is a device that presses your name, return address, seal, business, or monogram into your envelopes, stationery, or gifts and adds a bit of luxury. A handheld embosser is also a one-of-a-kind gift at an affordable price and is easily ordered online.

THE GOLDEN RULES FOR HANDWRITTEN SOCIAL AND SOCIAL MEDIA THANK-YOU SUCCESS

- **Don't go empty-handed:** When you are invited to someone's home for a party or dinner, always bring a gift to show your gratitude for the invitation. A bottle of wine, champagne, candles, a new set of dish towels, or even your favorite chocolate are all thoughtful ideas.
- **Make a phone call:** If you attend a dinner party at someone's home, remember to call your host the next day, then follow up with a handwritten thank-you note. If you feel it's a casual situation and an email or text would be more appropriate, that's fine, but remember, the personal touch of hearing your voice will always be appreciated.
- **When to send a note:** If someone invited you to attend an event "as their guest," be sure to send them a thank-you note within two weeks. A thank-you note would not be expected if you were invited to attend an event and you purchased your own ticket.
- **Be prepared:** Always have appropriate stationery on hand to use when you need it so your thank-you note is timely. Even better, if you've taken a great photo, print and send it with your thank-you note! Or you can consider uploading the party pics to one of the digital stationery apps that will allow you to include the image(s), write your note, hand-sign it, then send your thank-you note via postal mail for a nominal cost.
- **Virtual appreciation:** Some occasions have a strong social media presence where guests can contribute images, use hashtags, and comment to express their virtual thanks. Don't miss a wonderful opportunity to be together by being on your device the whole evening. Saying thank you on social media, in lieu of a personal thank-you, takes away the spirit, intimacy, and elegance of the handwritten note, so be sure to send the written note as well.
- **Consider the guest list before posting photos:** Before you post an image or video from a night out for everyone who *wasn't* included to see, do consider if there will be hurt feelings. Naturally, not all of your friends or followers can always make it, but when you post the pics, there will likely be someone who might feel left out of the group.

- **Get approval before you post pics:** Before you post photos to social media, try to get the blessing of everyone in the picture in order to avoid any embarrassment. The last thing you want is for someone to be upset over what you posted and ask you to remove it—especially when your intention was to celebrate what you thought was a great picture and wonderful time! Sometimes editing the image with a photo app or adding a filter will improve the candid shot and make everyone look good!

Jacqueline Kennedy Onassis's *Goodwill*

Jacqueline Kennedy Onassis had an incredibly full social calendar, but she presented herself to the world as an ambassador of goodwill with unforgettable grace and dignity. My mother, too, was a brilliant light. Volunteering her time for as long as I can remember—she spent countless hours organizing events like the Angel's Flight Gala to help runaway children. While spearheading charity drives and celebrity tournaments, working with the philanthropies of National Charity League, Inc., and the Los Angeles Orphanage Guild, she honored our veterans and the WWII heroes of the Mighty Eighth Air Force with the Heritage League of the Second Air Division. As I learned from her, I saw the utter joy and appreciation on the faces of people whose lives she directly impacted by her kindness. This truly affected and altered the course of my life. Honored on both coasts by the mayor of Albany, New York as a Tulip Princess, and by the City of Los Angeles as an Irish Woman of the Year—Honoree for her philanthropy in the community, she was a light of inspiration to us all and left an indelible handprint on our hearts. Share your smile, it may be the only positive energy someone sees in a day.

THANKS FOR HAVING ME—SAMPLE NOTES

It is essential to send a thank-you note for an event you have been invited to as a guest. Whether it be for a dinner, a weekend at someone's home, or an event, a note of thanks must be sent. On the following pages are some sample thank-you notes you can copy, fill in, or use for inspiration as you write your own.

THANKS FOR THE DINNER OR DINNER PARTY

Dear _____,

I just want to thank you again for the delicious dinner at your gorgeous home last evening. I so appreciate your attention to every detail and the love you put into everything you do. Please know I will remember this special night for a long time to come.

Sincerely yours,

_____

My dear _____,

In the words of Shakespeare, "Small cheer and great welcome makes a merry feast." Dinner was divine and the company even more exquisite. I so appreciate your graciousness and simply cannot wait to return.

A thousand thank-yous,

_____

Dear _____,

Nothing is more wonderful than breaking bread with the people you love and toasting to life. The wine, amazing food, and stimulating conversation created memories I will forever cherish. Here's to many more priceless moments! Thank you, thank you, thank you!

Love,

_____

. . . .

Dear _____,

It was so lovely to spend the evening with you and be in your presence. I could feel the love you put into every delicious dish you made for us last night—you must have spent weeks planning such an amazing party! Well, it was truly worth every single moment. It was a feast to remember, and I would like to be the first to return—I will even do the dishes!

My love and thanks to you,

_____

. . . .

Dear _____,

I woke up this morning laughing and dreaming about that amazing food you served last night! Oh my gosh, that (name of dish) was the hit of the party! Is there anything you can't do? Who knew you were an amazing (baker/chef)! I have to have that recipe or you must invite me back very soon. I really had the best time. Thank you so much for including me.

Kisses,

_____

THANKS FOR HOSTING THE POTLUCK PARTY

Dear _____,

What a wonderful idea to throw a dinner party and have everyone bring their favorite dish! It made the night so entertaining, and we felt proud to share our (favorite/secret/family) recipes with our friends. Thank you for bringing us together and creating a memorable evening.

Yours truly,

_____

THANKS FOR THE FABULOUS AFFAIR—EVENT, COMPANY, OR CHARITY

Dear _____,

The (name of event, tea party, luncheon, etc.) for (name of charity) was truly an event I will never forget. I deeply appreciated your inviting me to attend and allowing me the opportunity to see firsthand the work that is being done for this deserving cause. Please include me on the guest list for next year's fundraiser. Thank you again for such a moving day that left handprints on my heart.

Sincerely,

_____

Dear _____,

The (name of event) was utterly spectacular! I wish you my heartfelt congratulations on the success of (name of event, company, charity) and offer my sincere appreciation to you for (inviting me/including me) as your guest. It was truly a magical night.

Most sincerely,

_____

THANK YOU FOR THE EXHIBIT, CONCERT, OR SHOW

Dear _____,

I know that the tickets for (name of event) were sold out and difficult to get. I was thrilled when you (called or emailed) and (gave me your tickets or invited me to attend with you). Please know it was truly an experience I will never forget. Thank you for such a wonderful memory and the opportunity to enjoy this amazing night.

Sincerely yours,

_____

THANK YOU, GOVERNMENT OFFICIAL, FOR INVITING ME TO THE RECEPTION

Dear _____,

What a pleasure it was to make your acquaintance last evening at the (name of event) reception for (person's name). I truly admire the work you have done, and I hope our lawmakers look to your ideas to (official's project you admire). If there is anything I can do to support your mission, please let me know. Thank you for including me in this unforgettable night.

Respectfully yours,

_____

THANK YOU FOR THE WEEKEND AWAY

Dear _____,

My weekend at your home in (name of location) was simply magical. I can still smell the delicious (BBQ/dinner/breakfast/lunch) we had and taste that amazing (dessert/wine/etc.) How did the two of you become such incredible gourmet chefs? Please know I appreciated that you made me feel so welcome in every way. I look forward to seeing you both again soon.

Sincerely yours,

_____

THANK YOU FOR THE INVITATION—ACCEPT OR REGRET

If you are sending an email response, you could send something casual like this:

Dear _____,

I accept with pleasure your kind invitation to attend the celebration for (name of person)'s birthday on (day and date) at the (name of location) at (time of day). Thank you for including me in the festivities!

Most sincerely,

_____

Dear _____,

Thank you for the kind invitation to your party. Unfortunately, I am already committed for that evening and will be unable to attend. I appreciate your thinking of me and know it will be a wonderful celebration. Please keep me on your list for the next time.

Sincerely yours,

_____

CHAPTER 4

Personal MILESTONES and *Special* MOMENTS

THANKS FOR THE WONDERFUL MEMORIES

> 'THANK YOU' IS THE BEST PRAYER THAT ANYONE COULD SAY.
> I SAY THAT ONE A LOT. THANK YOU EXPRESSES EXTREME
> GRATITUDE, HUMILITY, UNDERSTANDING.
>
> —Alice Walker, American author

Every single moment in our lives is a blessing, but extra-special moments are a cut above. It is always essential to be mindful of the precious gift of being with those we love and honoring our successes in life. Whether you're graduating, celebrating a birthday, moving into a new home, marking a personal achievement, attending your first gala, or embarking on your next global tour, the good wishes—and, of course, the many thoughtful gifts from family and friends—make those remarkable moments in life truly special, creating memories that will last a lifetime. It only takes a few minutes to say thank you and show your appreciation for even the smallest way that someone supported you. So the next time you reach a personal milestone, let people know just how much their love and generosity mean to you.

> **I'VE LEARNED THAT PEOPLE WILL FORGET WHAT YOU SAID, PEOPLE WILL FORGET WHAT YOU DID, BUT PEOPLE WILL NEVER FORGET HOW YOU MADE THEM FEEL.**
>
> —Maya Angelou, American poet

TIPS FOR SAYING THANK YOU AFTER A SPECIAL OCCASION

- **Still say thank you:** Even if you thanked someone enthusiastically when you opened the gift, you should still send a thank-you note.
- **Say it from your heart:** Make your note personal and conversational; write it as if you were speaking with the person who gave you the gift.
- **Use stationery apps if you're in a pinch:** On the run and without paper and pen? Handwritten is always best, but if you want to use your computer or mobile device, check out stationery apps, which make sending a note effortless. Some apps allow you to write and personally sign your note, upload your party photo, access your contacts, and mail your thank-you as a postcard or note in an envelope for a small fee through the postal service.
- **Netiquette:** If you want to let your friend know you received their thoughtful gift and convey your excitement, of course you can share a post on social media or send a text, but the best way is to send a note of thanks.

Easy Etiquette

Celebrate your successes on social media! That's a wonderful place to announce your achievements and inspire others to rise up and fulfill their dreams!

> **THOUSANDS OF CANDLES CAN BE LIT FROM A SINGLE CANDLE, AND THE LIFE OF THE CANDLE WILL NOT BE SHORTENED. HAPPINESS NEVER DECREASES BY BEING SHARED.**
>
> —Buddha, enlightened teacher

THANKS FOR THE WONDERFUL MEMORIES—SAMPLE NOTES

Here are some sample notes to help you say thanks for the memories with elegance and impact.

THANK YOU FOR MY BIRTHDAY GIFT

Dear _____,

How very thoughtful of you to think of me on my birthday. I just love the (gift) and want you to know that every time I (wear it, see it, use it), I think of you. Thank you for all your generosity. I look forward to seeing you soon.

With all my love,

_____

. . . .

Dear _____,

The (gift) you gave me for my birthday is perfect! I love it! I know you put so much thought into finding something amazing, and that means the world to me. Thank you for making me feel so special!

With much love to you,

_____

Dear _____ ,

*Thank you for making my birthday unforgettable! I adore the (gift) you
gave me and will treasure it always. Thank you so very much for helping
me celebrate another fabulous year!*

Cheers,

_____

Easy Etiquette

The next time someone asks you for gift ideas, request personalized stationery;
then send that person a thank-you note on it!

Dear _____ ,

*Wow! What can I say, but thank you from the bottom of my heart for the
most amazing gift ever! I love the (gift) so much and look forward to (using
it, reading it, spending it, etc.). A million thanks!*

Hugs,

_____

Dear _____ ,

*Oh my gosh! How do you always find me the perfect gift? I love it! I am so
grateful for your thoughtfulness and for having you in my life. I adore you!*

Love,

_____

THANK YOU FOR THE BIRTHDAY GIFT CARD

Dear _____,

You always know the perfect thing to get me! Thank you so very much for the gift card to (name of store/restaurant). I promise you that I will immediately put it to good use. I really appreciate your kindness and generosity. Sending you a million hugs and kisses! XO

Love,

_____

> **WHEN YOU ARISE IN THE MORNING, THINK OF WHAT A PRIVILEGE IT IS TO BE ALIVE, TO BREATHE, TO THINK, TO ENJOY, TO LOVE.**
> —Marcus Aurelius, Roman philosopher

THANK YOU FOR THE SURPRISE BIRTHDAY PARTY

Dear _____,

Oh, you got me! I am still shocked! I thought everyone was acting strange, but I never imagined I was walking into my own surprise party. Please know it meant so much to me that you went to such great lengths to make sure I had a special celebration for my birthday. I will never forget your love and kindness—thank you from the bottom of my heart.

Gratefully yours,

_____

THANK YOU FOR SPENDING THE DAY WITH ME—BIRTHDAY

Dear _____,

*Thank you for spending the day with me and celebrating my birthday.
I had the most amazing time! More important, I am so grateful for the gift
of your love and friendship, which means the world to me. Thank you for
making this day something I will treasure for a lifetime.*

Lots of love,

_____

BON VOYAGE—MOVING TO COLLEGE, SEMESTER AWAY

Dear _____,

*I can't tell you how much I appreciated your being at my bon voyage
party to help send me off. I am really looking forward to going to (name of
country/name of college), but I will miss you desperately. I love the (name
of gift) and promise to text pictures of my adventures.*

*While my departure is bittersweet, thank you for making it très
magnifique! Au revoir!*

Merci,

_____

Easy Etiquette

If you are invited to a hosted event like a wedding or birthday party via an
online site, always respond by the RSVP date or within a few days of receiving
the invitation so your host can plan accordingly. Remember, when someone
invites you to be their guest, they should not have to keep following up to see if
you are attending.

THANK YOU FOR THE VIRTUAL BIRTHDAY CELEBRATION

Dear _____,

You are simply amazing! Here I was, wishing we could get together and thinking how tough it would be to not celebrate with everyone in person! It was so much fun to get a birthday (drop-off/delivery) (box/party bag) filled with so many fun things, connect with everyone, and catch up. What a great idea. You really made me feel like a rock star! It meant the world to me to be celebrated in such a sweet way. Thank you for making my birthday so magical and making my wishes come true.

Love,

_____

THANK YOU, PARENT(S)/GRANDPARENT(S) FOR MY SPECTACULAR GIFT

Dear _____,

There are simply no words to express how deeply I appreciate your (helping me buy/buying me) (name of spectacular gift)! I never imagined that (on my birthday/graduation/just because) my dream would come true. I know you have worked so hard to give me this, and in return, I want you to know that I will continue to focus on my (schoolwork/career/other efforts). Thank you for always believing in me and having confidence in my dreams.

With all my love, always,

_____

THANKS FOR THE DONATION TO MY CHARITY FUNDRAISER

Dear _____,

It is with my profound appreciation that I thank you from the bottom of my heart for your generous contribution to (name of charity). Your donation will not only change lives but allow this important work to carry on in our community and inspire others to make a difference. It is these random acts of kindness, big or small, that effect change and promote a spirit of goodwill worldwide.

My sincerest gratitude,

_____

THANKS FOR COMING TO MY DEBUTANTE OR CHARITY BALL

Dear _____,

It was such an honor to have you at my (debutante/charity) ball last Saturday evening to celebrate our philanthropic efforts in the community. Your presence was a gift in itself, but please know I so appreciated your donation in support of (favorite charity). Thank you for sharing this unforgettable evening with me and joining me in the effort to make a difference in our world.

My sincere thanks,

_____

THANKS FOR THE FABULOUS GRADUATION GIFT—WISH YOU WERE HERE!

Dear _____,

It was so generous of you to send me a check for my graduation from (name of school). Although I wished you were here, I knew that all your good wishes were with me as I received my diploma. I so appreciate the (gift card/money) you sent, and I plan on (putting it to good use/using it to pay off my student loans/getting a new computer/buying a suit for my first job interview). I would love to celebrate the next time we're together. Thank you for your thoughtfulness.

Lots of love,

_____

THANKS, PROFESSOR, FROM A GRATEFUL GRADUATE

Dear Professor _____,

I can't believe that the moment I have worked so hard for has finally arrived. While I am excited to graduate and move on to the next chapter of my life, it is also bittersweet. You have influenced my life decisions, broadened my horizons, and encouraged me to reach further than I ever dreamed I could. Thank you for making a difference in my life…I will remember your words of wisdom always.

Most sincerely,

_____

THANKS FOR COMING TO MY GRADUATION

Dear _____,

It meant so much to me to have you at my graduation. Looking out into the audience and seeing you cheering as I received my diploma was a moment I will forever cherish. From my heart, I thank you for sharing this personal achievement with me and encouraging me to challenge myself. Thank you for believing I could do it.

With affection,

_____

Easy Etiquette

Even if you send out or receive a graduation announcement card, a gift isn't required in return.

THANK YOU TO MY PARENTS FOR SUPPORTING MY COLLEGE DREAMS

Dear _____,

What can I say but thank you, thank you, thank you—for always supporting me along my journey of life and insisting that the foundation be a good education. Thank you for never letting me quit, for believing that I could do anything, and giving me the tools to help me leave my mark on this world. Yes, I did it—but I couldn't have done it without your support. I love you both and am forever grateful.

With all my love,

_____

THANK YOU FOR HELPING ME MOVE

Dear _____,

No way could I ever have moved into my new apartment without your help! Thank you for helping me pack, carry boxes, bags, and everything in between, and for doing it in such good spirits. I would love to have you back for dinner to show my appreciation, so please let me know when you have a free night in the coming weeks. Thank you!

Gratefully yours,

_____

THANK YOU FOR WARMING MY NEW HOME

Dear _____,

Thank you so much for coming over and helping me celebrate my new home! I loved (name of kitchen gift) and simply can't wait to enjoy my new kitchen. Now that I have a place to call my own, I will definitely be spending time developing my culinary skills, and you must come back. Until then, thanks ever so much!

Love,

_____

> THE MEANING OF LIFE IS TO FIND YOUR GIFT.
> THE PURPOSE OF LIFE IS TO GIVE IT AWAY.
>
> —Pablo Picasso, Spanish painter

CHAPTER 5

Professional
CORRESPONDENCE
CLIMBING THE LADDER OF SUCCESS

> WHEN YOU DO GOOD, YOU GET GOOD! FULFILMENT COMES FROM SERVING OTHERS, NOT JUST HUSTLING TO SERVE YOURSELF. ON THE PATH TO SUCCESS, THERE IS ALWAYS GOING TO BE AN OPPORTUNITY TO HELP SOMEONE ELSE BE SUCCESSFUL TOO. TAKE THAT OPPORTUNITY, AND BE THE KIND OF PERSON WHO MAKES A DIFFERENCE IN THE LIVES OF OTHERS.

—Denzel Washington, American actor

The ability to write a gracious and memorable thank-you note has advantages that extend far beyond the social world—it can actually make a huge difference in getting your dream job or creating a thriving company. In today's competitive marketplace, large corporations and small business owners know the benefit of thanking their clients for their patronage. It's that personal connection of saying, "We appreciate your business" that brings customers back, creating the possibility of a continued relationship.

On a personal level, a successful business also involves maintaining good professional relationships with the people you meet along the way and ensuring they know how appreciative you are for their time and support. Professional correspondence is key, especially following a job interview. Not only does it show the interviewer that you have good manners, but it also helps you stand out from the crowd of other candidates. Even if you don't get the job, sending a good-natured thank-you note reiterating your interest can turn rejection into a new possibility for success, should the situation change. So the next time you're planning to take a step up the ladder of success, remember to thank the people who supported or recommended your business.

Easy Etiquette

Life is too short to stay in a job you don't enjoy. Challenge yourself, have imagination, and create your own magic.

66 THERE IS ALWAYS ROOM AT THE TOP. 99
—Daniel Webster, American orator and statesman

WHEN TO SEND A THANK-YOU NOTE AFTER A JOB INTERVIEW

Send a handwritten, computer-generated, or emailed thank-you note following a job interview no later than two business days after the interview. An immediate follow-up to your meeting shows that you would make a conscientious and productive employee, executive, consultant, or vendor. Here are a few tips to remember:

- Send a note to any person who spoke on your behalf, referred you for a position, or wrote a letter of recommendation for you. If you don't personally thank someone who helped you, they may not help you again.
- If you are unsure if the interviewer is working remotely, simply send an email thank-you note.

- If you aren't chosen for the position you applied for, send a thank-you note reiterating your interest should another opportunity become available later down the road. Always thank them for the opportunity.
- If company circumstances change and the job is no longer available, thank your contacts for taking the time to speak with you and ask if they would be kind enough to forward your resume if they hear of any potential opportunities.
- If you are offered the position and elect *not* to accept the job, it is always best to send a thank-you note thanking them for the opportunity. They will appreciate your consideration, and it will leave the door open in the event you might like to work at this business in the future.

Easy Etiquette

A wonderful way to thank a client, friend, or coworker in a small but polite way is to take the person out for coffee. Coffee gift cards are an affordable alternative and an excellent idea to include with your thank-you note or to send via email.

HOW TO WRITE AN INTERVIEW THANK-YOU NOTE

Writing a thank-you note after you meet with a potential employer opens the door for further communication and gives you the ability to add one more positive point to your interview. How well you write your thank-you note will reflect how you present yourself and how you would represent their company. More important, you are demonstrating that you are intelligent enough to recognize that gratitude is an important asset in any business, and that you are a person with excellent values and social grace. Here are some additional tips:

- **The computer-generated or emailed thank-you note** is the most common format in the business world. Use a professional-looking letterhead when writing a thank-you note on your digital device. You can search your word-processing program for "business letters" templates.
- **When sending a handwritten** professional thank-you note, make sure to follow the guidelines in Chapter 1: Thank-You Notes 101.
- **Keep your note concise and limited to one page.** Always be sincere and professional in what you write. Know your audience and maintain the appropriate level of formality in your salutation and closing. There's no need to restate your resume, so use this note as an opportunity to express any additional ideas you might have or to add something you forgot to say in the interview.
- **Reiterate your desire for the position, clarify any uncertainties the interviewer might have expressed, and show your strengths.** Do say, "I will follow up with you next week."
- **Include all the key pieces of information, including** the date and company contact information, as well as your professional contact information, *LinkedIn* link, website, social media, or other branding information. If you don't want to include your home address, you don't need to. Telephone and email communication is always the preferred method for professional contact.
- **Double-check that you have the correct spelling of the person's name.** Would you hire someone who spelled your name wrong in a thank-you note?
- **Proofread your letter.** Always read it out loud and use the spell-check option in your word-processing or email program. Check for punctuation, proper capitalization and spacing, and autocorrect errors. You don't want to lose a job offer simply because you were sloppy.
- **Your signature should be handwritten** in black or blue ink for computer-generated notes—it adds a personal touch.
- **Always use an envelope that matches your stationery.** If you are printing your thank-you note, the envelope should be printed as well. Refer to Chapter 1 for all the details on formatting business envelopes.

Your professional thank-you note printed from your computer and sent through the mail should look like this:

February 6, 20___ (date at the top of the page)

Ms. Ashton Taylor
Innovation Digital
316 West 42nd Street
New York, NY 10019

Dear Ms. Taylor: (use a colon here instead of a comma)

I wanted to take a moment to thank you for meeting with me this afternoon. I really appreciate the generous time you took to look at my work. Should a position become available I would be thrilled to join your team. Please find below the website link to my online portfolio and *LinkedIn* profile. Thank you again. I look forward to hearing from you soon.

Sincerely,

Riley Jones
she/her (pronoun preference)
(mobile number—if you wish to include it)
(*LinkedIn* profile link)
(website address)
(social media links—only if you use them professionally)

UNDERSTANDING, USING, AND RESPECTING PERSONAL PRONOUNS

Using an honorific ahead of someone's name indicates your respect for their marital or professional status. For example, when a professional woman chooses to use the honorific "Ms."—which does not indicate whether she is married or single—the message is clear: Her personal life is private. You should use a person's preference in correspondence.

Think of personal pronouns (*he*, *she*, *they*, and so on) in the same way—they are connected to our identity, empower us to live our lives to their fullest, and must be honored. You can share your preferred pronouns with others to indicate how you would like to be identified and addressed. Likewise, if someone has clearly indicated their personal pronoun to you, it is how they want to be recognized and respected in all forms of communication and is important to their sense of self. Here's what you need to know to embrace modern personal pronoun use and create an inclusive environment:

- The practice of including your preferred pronouns following or under your name is universally accepted across business and personal communication and social media sites.
- Identifying your personal pronouns can help avoid hurt feelings that may happen as a result of gender misidentification.
- Personal pronouns can be displayed in either uppercase or lowercase, with or without parentheses, or styled in a lighter font. The choice is up to you.
- Common personal pronouns include but are not limited to:
  - *she/her*
  - *he/him/his*
  - *they/them*

- Adding your gender profile to your company email signature is a wonderful opportunity to build diversity and inclusion professionally, creating a conscious display of support for yourself or your team.

- Consider using your pronoun alongside or under your email signature, on your business card, or on your name tag or identification badge, like in these examples:

  - Morgan Smith he/his
  - Morgan Smith she/her
  - Morgan Smith (they/them/theirs)
  - Morgan Smith
    they/them

> 66 MY LIFE DIDN'T PLEASE ME, SO I CREATED MY LIFE. 99
>
> —Coco Chanel, French fashion designer

Easy Etiquette

According to etiquette expert Dorothea Johnson, author and founder of The Protocol School of Washington®, "Ms." is the correct honorific for a woman in the business arena, regardless of what she chooses to call herself in her private life, unless she has specified otherwise. Revived by twentieth-century feminists, "Ms." has been around since at least the seventeenth century as an abbreviation for the honorific "Mistress," which applied to both married and unmarried women, and from which both "Miss" and "Mrs." derive.

THE BUSINESS STATIONERY CHECKLIST

When sending a business thank-you note, your choice of paper creates another opportunity to express your elegance, creativity, and success. Keep these tips in mind when choosing your professional stationery:

- Use paper that is a higher quality than regular white copy paper. Standard business-size $8\frac{1}{2}$" × 11" sheets are available in watermarked, 100 percent cotton paper in ecru or white with a coordinating envelope. Stay away from colors.
- Monarch sheets or executive sheets are smaller and are available in $7\frac{1}{4}$" × $10\frac{1}{2}$" size. These are perfect for the personal business note and fit easily through a printer if necessary.
- The business correspondence card size is $4\frac{1}{2}$" × $6\frac{1}{2}$" and is a heavier card stock. These cards are used for occasions that are professional but a bit more personal.
- If you write a lot of professional notes, order customized letterhead and envelopes with your name and address, or create your own on the computer.
- Online sites and office supply stores carry Crane & Co. letter-size business paper with matching envelopes for your thank-you notes, correspondence, cover letter, and resume. Visit www.crane.com to view the online selections.

Easy Etiquette

For personal security, don't include your home address on your resume and use your mobile phone number and/or email address as a contact. This is a good point to consider if you post your resume with a headhunter or on job resource websites where your email should be a sufficient form of contact.

The Business *Thank-You* Thesaurus

Use a thesaurus; you can find many ways to say the same thing, only better! Most word programs have a built-in thesaurus. Here are some words that could help you write job interview thank-you notes:

ABILITY	CULTURED	INSPIRATION	SPECIALIST
ACCOMPLISHED	DEDICATED	KNOWLEDGEABLE	STYLISH
AFICIONADO	DEVOTED	POWER	TALENTED
AUTHORITY	EDUCATED	PRACTICED	TECHNICALLY
BRILLIANT	ENTHUSIASTIC	PROFESSIONAL	VETERAN
CAPABLE	EQUIPPED	PROFICIENT	WELL-INFORMED
CLOUT	EXPERIENCED	QUALIFIED	WELL-READ
COMMITTED	EXPERT	REFINED	WELL-TRAVELED
COMPETENT	FAMILIAR	SAVVY	WIZ
CONNOISSEUR	FIT	SKILLED	
CONSULTANT	GIFTED	SKILLFUL	
CREATIVE	INFLUENCE	SOPHISTICATED	

VIRTUAL GRATITUDE: THE FUNDAMENTALS OF THANK-YOU NOTE NETIQUETTE

Many corporations today prefer using email for the majority of their business. It makes sense, then, that many companies readily accept this form of a thank-you note for interviews, meetings, business lunches, and dinners because it is efficient, cost-effective, professional, and instantaneous, and it provides access to someone you might not have had contact with otherwise. Whether or not you send an email thank-you note is really a matter of discretion, so use your best judgment. The advantage of email is that it is immediately received by your interviewer.

Email Thank-You Note Checklist

In addition to following the basic rules of writing the business note, an email thank-you to your interviewer must look professional; be well thought out; and avoid the use of acronyms, emoticons, and slang. For example, never include acronyms like "TY" for *thank you*. Here are some other tips for sending an email thank-you:

- **Don't run home and send your emailed thank-you note right away.** Wait a few hours or a day later. The objective is to remind them of you, so don't act *too* quickly.
- **Include a clear subject line.** Keep in mind that your thank-you note could be caught by a spam filter, so make sure you include a few words in your subject line like "Thank You for the Interview." Double-check the email address before you send it.
- **Maintain a professional email address.** You don't want to lose a job opportunity because your interviewer feels your email address is inappropriate. Using your name, initials, or a combination of both is always a good option. If your choice isn't available, try using a period or underscore between your name, like this: Your.Name@email.com.

Proper Email Formatting

The format of an emailed thank-you note is really a blend of the handwritten and the business notes. Because the addressee's email is already included, there's no need to rewrite it in the body of the message. Typically, the email thank-you includes your salutation, followed by the person's name, your thank-you message, the closing, and your name, followed by your contact information. It should look like this:

To: Ashton.Taylor@company.com

From: Riley.Jones@email.com

Date: 2-15-20___ 9:00AM PST

Subject: Thank You for the Interview

Dear Mr. Taylor:

I just wanted to follow up and let you know how much I appreciated meeting with you yesterday. It would be such an honor for me to work at (COMPANY NAME) and be a part of the development of (technology/business/creative). Should an innovation position become available on your (kind of) team, please let me know. Thank you again for taking the time to meet with me.

Sincerely,
Riley Jones (she/her)
(415) 555-1212—mobile
Website Link—*LinkedIn* URL—Social Media

> 66 GRATITUDE IS A WAY TO A DEEPER WISDOM. LOOK FOR THAT DEEPER WISDOM; BELIEVE ME, THERE'S A GREAT HUNGER FOR IT. AND HERE YOU'RE IN LUCK. AS AMERICANS, YOU HAVE A SPECIAL CLAIM TO IT. 99
>
> —Ronald Reagan, fortieth US president, Presidential Scholar Awards, 1988

GLOBAL GRATITUDE BUSINESS TIPS

With the evolution of globalization, protocol has become a highly sophisticated and strategic asset in today's business, military, and diplomatic world. Keep in mind these leadership tips from Pamela Eyring, president of The Protocol School of Washington®, for supporting international relations and being a universal role model. For more information, visit www.psow.edu.

- Self-awareness of your own professional behavior is critical when building relationships at work. Always treat everyone with respect. Also, pay attention to how someone treats others; it's a true indicator of how they will treat you.
- When building your business relationships around the world, make sure to do in-depth research on the customs and business protocol specific to the countries you are working in. Tip: If you are not comfortable shaking hands, put your hand over your heart as soon as you walk into the interview to signal your greeting.
- Remember that "please" and "thank you" go a long way toward promoting civility and mutual respect.

TIPS FOR BUSINESS OWNERS: HOW TO SAY THANK YOU TO YOUR EMPLOYEES AND CUSTOMERS

Whether your business is global or consists of a small group of clients, the fact remains that your customers appreciate being thanked for their continued loyalty. In our tech-savvy world, the personal touch can make all the difference in the growth and success of your business. Thanking your clients can promote a deeper sense of loyalty to you, increase business, and help secure referrals. Equally important is thanking the people who work for you. You will benefit when you thank them for their work and recognize their dedication. After all, they are contributing to your success. It's also important for you to model the kind of behavior you would like your staff to project. If you give the gift of gratitude, you will receive it in return.

In this arena, there are limitless ways to show your appreciation:

- Provide your employees with high-quality thank-you cards so they can send handwritten notes to all their best customers. The personal touch will help you stand out from your competitors. Remember, always include your business card with your note.
- Send thank-you notes when people do something thoughtful for you, such as referring business, taking you to lunch or dinner, sending you a gift, or giving you tickets to an event.
- Send cards to your best clients all year-round, not just for the holidays, to thank them for their continued patronage. For your most important clients, consider gifting them tickets to sporting events or the theater, gift baskets, bottles of wine, or gift cards.
- Unite your team and host a lunch to publicly recognize a good quality of each of your associates and express how much you appreciate their time and energy. A small token of your gratitude can help keep spirits high and your employees happy. Remember, they represent your brand to the world.
- Always *personally* thank every single person who works for you. Everyone's job is integral to your success, and it's important for each person to feel acknowledged. Whether on their birthday or at the end of the year, many employees hope for a gift or bonus that shows your appreciation for their efforts.

THANKS FOR THE JOB OPPORTUNITY—SAMPLE NOTES

Customize any of these thank-you notes to suit your personal needs!

THANK YOU FOR THE INTERVIEW

Dear _____:

I just want to follow up on my interview with you today and let you know how much I appreciate your taking the time to meet with me. During our conversation, you mentioned several projects (name of company) is currently working on. It would be my pleasure to put some ideas together to present to you or integrate some ideas or approaches. I look forward to hearing from you at your earliest convenience.

Sincerely,

_____

THANK YOU FOR SPEAKING ON MY BEHALF

Dear _____:

It meant the world to me that you took the time to speak on my behalf. Please know that not only do I appreciate your interrupting your busy day to help someone else; I value the kind words you said about me as well. Thank you!

Sincerely,

_____

THANK YOU FOR LOOKING AT MY PROJECT/SCRIPT/ PROPOSAL

Dear _____:

Per our conversation, please find enclosed (project name/script title/ proposal) for your consideration. I appreciate your taking the time to read it, and I look forward to hearing your thoughts. If you have any questions, please don't hesitate to contact me.

Sincerely,

_____

Dear _____:

Thank you for returning my material with your notes and ideas. It isn't often that someone takes the time to go the extra mile, and I appreciate all your effort to help me. I'd love to keep the door open to send you my (projects/scripts/proposals) in the future. A thousand thanks.

Best regards,

_____

THANK YOU FOR THE INTERVIEW—WHEN YOU DID NOT GET AN OFFER

Dear _____:

Thank you for updating me on the position at (business name). Please know that if anything should change or if a new position becomes available, I would be interested in returning to meet with you. Thank you again for your time and consideration.

Sincerely,

_____

THANK YOU FOR THE OFFER, BUT...

Dear _____:

It was an honor to receive your call offering me the position at (company name). While I know working with you would be a wonderful experience, I have chosen to pursue another opportunity at this time. Thank you very much for your consideration. I wish you the best of luck in finding the right candidate for the position.

Sincerely,

_____

THANKS FOR THE BUSINESS OPPORTUNITY—SAMPLE NOTES

Following are samples that business owners can use to communicate with employees and customers.

THANKS FOR HELPING MAKE THE COMPANY A SUCCESS—EMPLOYEE

Dear _____:

As a small token of thanks for your hard work and continued loyalty at (name of business), please find enclosed a gift card to (store/restaurant/ hotel). We recognize your dedication, and we truly appreciate valuable associates like you. Thank you for contributing to our success.

Most sincerely,

_____

THANK YOU FOR YOUR CUSTOMER LOYALTY

Dear _____:

Thank you for the confidence you have placed in us. We are a company dedicated to excellence in customer service, and your satisfaction is our top priority. Please let us know if we can be of any further assistance to you. We appreciate your trust.

Sincerely yours,

_____

Dear _____,

You have been a loyal customer of ours for the past (number of months/ years), and to show our appreciation we'd like to present you with the enclosed (gift card/coupon) to be used on (Customer Appreciation Day/ your next purchase/at your convenience). Thank you for being a part of the (name of company) family.

Sincerely,

_____ (name of president/owner)

THANK YOU FOR THE BUSINESS LUNCH OR DINNER— CLIENT OR BUSINESS ASSOCIATE

Dear _____:

What a pleasure it was to meet with you over lunch this afternoon. I think we accomplished a great deal, and I look forward to working together. If you have any further questions or concerns, please let me know. Thank you again for the excellent meal and conversation.

Sincerely,

_____

THANK YOU FOR THE BUSINESS GIFT

Dear _____:

When your gift arrived at the office today, everyone cheered and congregated in the conference room. I have never seen a group of dignified people tear through (food item) in such a short amount of time. Thank you for the very thoughtful and delicious gift.

Sincerely,

_____

THANK YOU FOR YOUR CHARITABLE DONATION—FROM A NONPROFIT

Dear _____:

Thank you for your charitable donation to (name of charity). It is because of generous gifts from good-hearted people like you that we are able to make a significant difference in the lives of so many (children/people/ seniors). Your contribution will be used to (briefly mention use). From the bottom of our hearts to yours, we thank you.

Sincerely,

_____

THANK YOU FOR VOLUNTEERING—FROM A NONPROFIT

Dear _____,

On behalf of (name of charity), we would like to extend our profound gratitude to you for all of the time, love, and effort you have selflessly given to our organization to make our world a better place. Thank you for sharing your bright light, generous spirit, and helping us change lives.

With our sincere appreciation,

_____

Easy Etiquette

"Best regards" is the most common closing to use for correspondence in the entertainment industry.

COLLEGE INTERVIEW THANK-YOU NOTES

Your choice of school can have a profound effect on the rest of your life. Here, too, the thank-you note can make a difference, so be sure to send one within two days of your college interviews. Remember, thousands of people are applying for those few slots. It's possible that you could secure a spot based on the fact that you followed up and demonstrated responsibility, civility, and determination. Sending a thank-you note sets you apart and gives you a great opportunity to reiterate how much you want to receive an acceptance letter.

It's also important to write thank-you notes to all the people who wrote letters of recommendation for you. If they took time to help you, they deserve to be thanked.

THANK YOU FOR THE COLLEGE INTERVIEW

Dear _____:

Thank you again for taking the time to meet with me yesterday and sharing your wonderful experiences as an alumnus of (name of college). I appreciated your advice and direction regarding the (Undergraduate Program/Master's Program/School of Focus/scholarship awards) and am excited about the possibility of attending. Thank you for giving me the opportunity to interview with you, and please don't hesitate to contact me if there is any additional information you might need.

Most sincerely,

_____

THANK YOU FOR THE LETTER OF RECOMMENDATION

Dear Professor _____:

I am so extremely grateful to you for writing a letter of recommendation on my behalf. You are someone I hold in high regard and view with a tremendous amount of respect. Please know how much I appreciate your endorsement. I hope to use it not only for graduate school applications but in the business world as well. Thank you.

Most sincerely,

_____

> 66 WHAT WE HAVE DONE FOR OURSELVES ALONE DIES WITH US;
> WHAT WE HAVE DONE FOR OTHERS AND THE WORLD
> REMAINS AND IS IMMORTAL. 99
>
> —Albert Pike, American author

CHAPTER 6

FRIENDS and SUPPORT *Circles*

THANK YOU FOR BEING A FRIEND

> **"FOR BEAUTIFUL EYES, LOOK FOR THE GOOD IN OTHERS; FOR BEAUTIFUL LIPS, SPEAK ONLY WORDS OF KINDNESS; AND FOR POISE, WALK WITH THE KNOWLEDGE THAT YOU ARE NEVER ALONE."**
>
> —Audrey Hepburn, Belgian-born actor

Sometimes the most precious gifts don't come in a box tied up with a beautiful bow but are intangible gestures of love and support wrapped in the fabric of the heart. Whether you're going through a bad breakup, recovering from a loss, or embarking on a new adventure or an exciting phase of life, the gifts of kindness, friendship, and understanding are what make our lives richer and sweeter. So the next time you've *gotten through* with a little help from your friends, let them know how grateful you are for their understanding.

When someone has done something nice for you, a great way to say thank you is to pay the kindness forward and pass the magic of gratitude on to someone else.

HOW TO THANK A FRIEND

It's true that handwritten notes are always best, but when it comes to friendship, saying thank you can take many forms beyond the formalities of pen and paper and social protocol. Often it is the unexpected thank-you that warms our hearts and touches our souls. Here are some ideas:

- **Handwritten cards and notes** sent through the mail often surprise the recipient with a burst of appreciation because they really are thoughtful and intimate. Try including a poetic quote on friendship with your thank-you note. Those poets really do have a way with words!

- **Playlists** are a fun way to share your gratitude with your friends. Think about what songs speak your message and transport you back to that moment when someone made a significant difference in your life. Text your bestie the link to the song so they can experience it with you. "Hey, every time I hear this song—I think of you...so grateful to have you in my life. XO."

- **Small gifts** make excellent thank-yous and need not be expensive. Who doesn't adore gorgeous flowers, fragrant candles, or festive champagne? These are always sweet thank-you options! If your friend loves to garden, a small package of flower seeds slipped into a card really shows your thoughtfulness.

- **Edible thank-yous** are delicious, whether home baked or from the corner bakery or candy shop. A small flat bar of your favorite chocolate fits perfectly in most envelopes!

- **Digital cards** are always kind, especially those created with one of the dozens of stationery sites that include music and animation. Check out Hallmark, American Greetings, and Blue Mountain. You'll find some amazing heartfelt and hilarious options to choose from.
- **Stationery apps** let you upload your favorite image of you and your friend and add a note and send a postcard or letter with your handwritten signature. This is a great way to print the picture that says a thousand words!

Easy Etiquette

L'Chaim—In Hebrew it means "to life"! Celebrate your laugh lines and embrace your wrinkles! They are outward signs of the smiles you have given to others and the joy you have expressed along your life's journey. Be grateful for every single breath you take, treasure each day the sun rises, and share your magic.

SPIRITUAL WAYS TO SHOW GRATITUDE

No matter what your spiritual preference, it's always a good idea to show gratitude to whatever higher power resonates with you. Embrace your faith and enrich your life with a daily practice of simply saying thank you to that divine force.

- Post a prayer or quote that inspires you to embrace all the blessings in your life on your bathroom mirror.
- Create a playlist of go-to songs that lift your soul and elevate your mood with good vibes. Soulful songs are like musical prayers that allow you to sing your praise.

- Prayers, verses, and meditations are common among many organized religious practices. Most important is the act of acknowledging your gratitude to whomever is your guiding force. Whatever positive thoughts and words that nurture your soul are the ones that are most important.
- Practice gratitude in what you say and do. Praying or sharing verses or quotes on your social media is one thing, but actually being a good person, showing love, kindness, and respect in what you say and do is the true spiritual key to enlightenment. Let peace begin within you.

> **LET GRATITUDE BE THE PILLOW UPON WHICH YOU KNEEL TO SAY YOUR NIGHTLY PRAYER.**
> —Maya Angelou, American poet

THANK YOU FOR BEING A FRIEND—SAMPLE NOTES

Here you will find notes to help you reach out and touch someone who has lifted you up. Use these words to show your appreciation for the people who have helped you through the rough patches in life.

THANKS FOR BEING THERE

Dear _____,

How can I ever thank you for always being there for me? You are a true friend, and I am forever grateful. Thank you.

With appreciation,

_____

THANKS FOR YOUR ENCOURAGEMENT

Dear _____,

Thank you for all of your words and texts of encouragement and support over these last few weeks. While I know "this, too, shall pass," it is friends like you that really lift us up and hold our hands along the way. Could not have walked this journey without your love, light, and kindness.

Forever grateful,

_____

> **❝I COUNT MYSELF IN NOTHING ELSE SO HAPPY AS IN A SOUL REMEMBERING MY GOOD FRIENDS.❞**
>
> —William Shakespeare, English playwright, *King Richard II*

THANKS FOR BEING MY SOUL SISTER

Dear _____,

We've laughed until we've cried and we've held each other tightly. I feel so blessed that we've walked this life together and shared in each other's joys and sorrows. From the bottom of my heart, thank you for being my soul sister and my best friend.

Love,

_____

THANKS FOR OUR ROCK-SOLID FRIENDSHIP

Dear _____,

You are the best! No matter what's happening, you are always someone I can count on through thick and thin. I don't think you'll ever know how much I appreciate your gracious heart and the courageous spirit that always makes me smile. You have affected my life on so many levels. I am truly a better person because of you. Thank you!

Yours truly,

_____

THANKS FOR HELPING ME THROUGH A TOUGH TIME

Dear _____,

Thank you for holding me up when I didn't think I was going to make it. Thank you for showing me there really is a light at the end of the tunnel. Thank you for reminding me to count my blessings. Thank you for explaining that time heals all wounds. Thank you for just letting me cry and not judging me for it. From my heart, I thank you, my friend.

Love,

_____

THANKS, JUST BECAUSE

Dear _____,

I want you to know that you mean the world to me. Thank you for walking the journey with me and simply being my very best friend.

With my love,

_____

Dear _____,

There are simply no words to express the depth of my gratitude...

Thank you,

_____

THANKS FOR BEING MY GREEK SISTER/BROTHER—COLLEGE LIFE

Dear _____,

It has been both an honor and a privilege to be your (name of fraternity) (sister/brother). Through all the exchanges, excitement, studying, and fraternity activity, you are someone I know will always be there for me. Thank you for being in my life.

Love,

_____

> NEVER SHALL I FORGET THE DAYS I SPENT WITH YOU. CONTINUE TO BE MY FRIEND, AS YOU WILL ALWAYS FIND ME YOURS.
>
> —Ludwig van Beethoven, German composer

CHAPTER 7

Love and ROMANCE

THANK YOU FROM THE BOTTOM OF MY HEART

> **"** YOU HAVE BEWITCHED ME BODY AND SOUL, AND
> I LOVE, I LOVE, I LOVE YOU. AND WISH FROM THIS DAY FORTH
> NEVER TO BE PARTED FROM YOU. **"**

—Mr. Darcy, Deborah Moggach, *Pride & Prejudice* screenplay

There is no doubt that one of our greatest human needs is to be loved by another and to experience the exhilarating feeling of appreciation. Romantic scribes know that the key to capturing a loved one's heart often begins with a passionate letter declaring their love and desire. With stars in their eyes, lovers bare their souls, risking rejection to give the gift of gratitude to another hopeful heart. Essentially, a love letter is like a declaration to thank someone for how they make you feel—their compassionate support, devoted understanding, or the sparkling electricity they feel in your presence.

In today's fast-paced world, we sometimes take each other for granted. Taking a moment to acknowledge the importance of the loves in our lives is essential—for both of you. Those two small words—thank you—are powerful, as they can create, break, or reinforce a relationship. Expressing your appreciation to the ones you adore should be a daily part of your mindful gratitude, as it is a practice critical to your own wellness. So the next time someone has touched your heart and you think you have finally found your one and only, send them a "Thank You from the Bottom of My Heart" note. It's guaranteed to create fireworks in their heart.

From the Bottom of *My Soul*—Love Note Phrases

I adore you...
I want you...
I need you...
I found you...finally.
I love you madly...
I love you deeply...
I treasure you...
From the bottom of my soul...
You are my first thought in the morning...
You are my north star...
You take my breath away...
You are the beating of my heart...
You're my everything...
Your smile sends me to my knees...
I will love you always + forever...
My love, I only wish I found you sooner...
I wish you could see yourself the way I see you...
I cherish every moment we have had together; here's to a million more...
I am who I am because of you...
What did I do to deserve you, my darling...
You make my life more wonderful...
You are sheer magic and pure love and my brilliant guiding light...
My life is (richer/sweeter) because of you...
As I child, when I looked to the stars, I knew you were looking at them too.
Always be mine...
You are my one and only...

WRITING THE ROMANTIC THANK-YOU

When it comes to writing tender notes of love and appreciation, there aren't any set rules. The most important thing is to simply write down your feelings. What matters are the passionate words that come from your heart. Sometimes it feels difficult to express what you feel, or you might feel ridiculous writing something that seems overly dramatic or too emotional. But just a few words can have a tremendous impact. You don't have to write pages—a loving phrase or a sweet term of endearment will do.

> 66 FOR IT WAS NOT INTO MY EAR YOU WHISPERED, BUT INTO MY HEART.
> IT WAS NOT MY LIPS YOU KISSED, BUT MY SOUL. 99
>
> —Judy Garland, American actor

IDEAS FOR KEEPING LOVE ALIVE IN YOUR LIFE

You don't have to wait for Valentine's Day to give your love a card—surprise them with a thoughtful note throughout the year. Here are some easy ways to show your affection and gratitude to your beloved:

- Send a handwritten thank-you love note on your favorite stationery with a quick spray of your favorite fragrance, and they'll surely think of you! There are hundreds of stationery options to choose from—from creative or funny store-bought cards to elegant, finely crafted, and handmade paper.
- Send an actual postcard or one via a digital stationery app with a picture of the two of you. Include a short little note, love quote, poem, or simply…XO.
- Emails and online e-cards to your partner's personal email are always appreciated—add some excitement to their inbox!
- Text messaging is an instant way to let that special someone know you are thinking of them.
- Slip a note into your sweetheart's bag, pocket, lunch box, suitcase, or car. Even an adoring note on the bathroom mirror will put a spring in their step. They'll be

taken by surprise when they discover it and will be grateful to know you took the time to do something special.

- Don't forget that your appreciation can extend beyond a written thank-you note! Hugs, kisses, holding hands, and eye contact are all ways to connect with that attitude of gratitude that should never, ever end. Actions really do speak louder than words!
- Use food as a language of love. Prepare a fabulous candlelight dinner, drop off a basket of homemade chocolate chip cookies, or make a seaside picnic to express your adoration.

Easy Etiquette

Marriage and family therapists Drs. Lew and Gloria Richfield, authors of *Together Forever: 125 Loving Ways to Have a Vital and Romantic Marriage*, advise people to "Mail a love letter to your partner. With a stamp. Love letters shouldn't stop just because you live at the same address."

> " TO LOVE IS TO BURN, TO BE ON FIRE. "
> —Jane Austen, English author

TIMING IS EVERYTHING

It is a good idea to demonstrate your feelings, otherwise you'd never know if the person you love feels the same way about you. The beginning of a relationship is always exciting, so take your time, court each other, and savor every moment. Too much "fan mail" early on may be perceived as being overwhelming, so just use your best judgment. After a few dates, it would be entirely appropriate to send a note saying something sweet like "Hey_____, I really enjoy hanging out and spending time with you—would you like to go out again?"

On the other hand, if you have no intention of seeing someone again following your first date, then let the verbal thank-you given at the end of the evening suffice. Don't text the next day thanking them again, because then they will assume you're interested. If they follow up for another date, simply let them know you appreciated the date without setting up a future one.

Either way, acknowledging the effort your potential love interest makes causes that magical gift of gratitude to continue. People want to *keep* giving when they feel appreciated for their efforts, because it makes them feel good inside. So whatever you decide to do to express your appreciation, be expansive, be creative, and do it well, so those love blessings keep coming to you!

> I FELL IN LOVE WITH HER COURAGE, HER SINCERITY, AND HER FLAMING SELF-RESPECT. AND IT'S THESE THINGS I'D BELIEVE IN, EVEN IF THE WHOLE WORLD INDULGED IN WILD SUSPICIONS THAT SHE WASN'T ALL SHE SHOULD BE. I LOVE HER AND IT IS THE BEGINNING OF EVERYTHING.
>
> —F. Scott Fitzgerald, American author

THANK YOU FROM THE BOTTOM OF MY HEART—SAMPLE NOTES

When it comes to love and romance, there's nothing like a well-timed thank-you note to let someone know you adore them.

THANK YOU FOR LOVING ME

Darling _____,

To thoughtful you, from thankful me! Thank you for leaving your (smile/handprint) on my heart.

Love,

_____ XOXO

Dear _____,

You make me feel like I'm the only one in this whole wide world. Thank you for loving me.

Love,

_____

. . . .

Dear _____,

How can I convey my appreciation for the love and magic you send my way?

Love,

_____

. . . .

My dear _____,

There are simply no words to express how grateful I am to have you in my life....

With all my love and affection,

_____

. . . .

Dear _____,

You are my everything. XOXO

Love,

_____

Sweet _____,

In your hands you hold my heart. I love you.

Love,

_____

THANK YOU FOR BEING MY BEST FRIEND

Dear _____,

Thank you for loving me for who I am and never, ever trying to change me. Thank you for allowing me the freedom to pursue my dreams and believing that I really can do anything. Thank you for applauding my victories and catching me when I fall. Thank you for being my best friend. I adore you.

Love,

_____

THANK YOU FOR THE FLOWERS

Dear _____,

What a wonderful surprise! When those beautiful flowers came down the hall, I really thought they were for someone else. They were so stunning, I couldn't believe it when they stopped at my desk—then I saw my name on the card. My heart pounded and swelled with emotion when I read your sweet words. Thank you for making me the most envied person in the office!

I love you too...
XOXO

_____

> WHEN I SAW YOU, I FELL IN LOVE, AND YOU SMILED BECAUSE YOU KNEW.
> —Arrigo Boito, Italian poet, *Falstaff*

THANK YOU, JUST BECAUSE

Dear _____,

When I was little, I dreamed about what you'd be like. I looked into the heavens every night and wondered where you were and when we'd meet. I begged the stars to keep you safe and for the moon to light your way to me. As I stand next to you now and gaze into your eyes, I am so incredibly thankful I met you that starry, starry night.

With all my love,

_____

THANK YOU TO YOUR PARTNER'S PARENTS

This kind of thank-you note has an air of higher formality than a casual love note.

Dear _____,

It's been such a pleasure getting to know both of you over the past year. I really appreciate your welcoming me into your home and always including me in your family plans. I especially enjoyed helping in the kitchen, being a part of the family, and cooking that delicious (name of holiday) dinner. Thank you for making me feel so special.

Sincerely yours,

_____

THANK YOU FOR THE GIFT

Dear _____,

I am forever grateful to you for your thoughtful and generous gift. I know it comes from your gracious heart to mine.

A thousand kisses...
Love,

_____

THANK YOU FOR THE ROOFTOP CHAMPAGNE

My dear _____ ,

When I said I always wished to have champagne over the lights of the city, I never dreamed it would come true. Sipping bubbles high atop a garden rooftop was an experience I'll never forget. Thank you for caring enough to make my dream come true. Here's to many more star-filled nights.

With affection,
_____ XO

THANK YOU FOR DINNER

Dear _____ ,

How do you always think of the most wonderful things to do? I loved having dinner with you last night at (name of place/beach/park). It was such a fun idea and I really, really enjoyed being with you. Thank you for making it an amazing evening.

With affection,

_____

THANK YOU FOR LOVING ME, GOODBYE

Dear _____ ,

This note is hard for me to write because I love you. I have felt so honored to have you in my life, and I am eternally grateful to have had the chance to know you. I wish our timing were different, because if we had met in another place and time, who knows what could have been? Thank you for loving me so much that you are willing to let me go. I will remember you always.

Love,

_____

CHAPTER 8

WEDDING BELLS and
Thank-Yous

I DO, I DO, AND THANK YOU TOO!

> "I ASK YOU TO PASS THROUGH LIFE AT MY SIDE—TO BE
> MY SECOND SELF, AND BEST EARTHLY COMPANION."
>
> —Charlotte Brontë, English author, *Jane Eyre*

From the moment brides and grooms say, "I do!" they are swept up into a wave of wedding traditions, rituals, parties, and presents—all of which require thank-you notes. If you are at this exciting time in your life, you have so much to be thankful for. From the engagement party to the bachelor and bachelorette parties, the showers, the wedding, the honeymoon, and beyond into the first year of marriage, you should offer your gratitude and appreciation for the support and generosity that you enjoy from your friends and family at this special time.

Celebrate your blessings of love and write your thank-yous together and continue that magical spirit of gratitude through your married lives!

THE GRATEFUL COUPLE'S GUIDE TO THANK-YOU SUCCESS

Perhaps the most important thing you can do to ensure that every gift and expression of goodwill is thanked properly is to be organized. There is no way in the world you will be able to remember who gave you what gift and when, unless you find some way to keep track. After the wedding, it is often difficult to be so organized. The last thing you want to think about on your honeymoon is the mountain of thank-you notes that need to be sent out upon your return. It can be utterly overwhelming. By taking a few simple steps *before* the big day, you can reduce the worry and feel free to dance the night away. Here are a few ideas to help you remember who gave you what, so you can savor your wedded bliss:

- **Look at your online wedding registry:** The easiest way to keep track of who gave you what gift is via an online wedding registry. Most store registries allow you to see who purchased registered items, along with their contact information. This is particularly valuable if a guest brings their gift to the wedding and the card is missing. (Refer to Chapter 2's section "Online Gift Registries and Thank-You Lists" for more information.) Some registries, like *Amazon*'s, allow you to create and send a digital thank-you note to the gift-giver via their platform.

- **Check your wedding website for tools:** Wedding websites allow you to upload your personal content, pictures, event details and manage guest RSVPs, gift registries, your thank-you notes, hashtags, and social media links with important updates. Keep in mind that posting a blanket thank-you on your website to everyone for the gifts they sent you does not replace thanking each person individually for their generosity.

- **Use your guest list:** Your guest list is an opportunity to make sure you have everyone accounted for. Many couples keep a spreadsheet with a row for each invited guest and columns for their pertinent contact information. Additional lines can be easily inserted with the list of gifts received and thank-you notes sent. You can also keep people's contact information updated on your digital devices for easy access or uploading—for example, to online stationery apps.

- **Have someone keep a list when opening gifts:** Whether you are celebrating in person or virtually, ask someone to help you keep a list of every gift you are opening along with the name of the person who gave it to you. A quick notation in your wedding journal, on the back of the gift note, or on a digital device can assist with keeping track of gifts received.

THE GRATEFUL BRIDE AND GROOM'S HANDWRITTEN THANK-YOU CHECKLIST

Try to write and mail a few thank-you notes every day so you don't get overwhelmed. Set aside time with your new spouse to write a few with you, and of course you can sign them together. Open a bottle of bubbly, order in, and make it fun. Count your blessings!

- Traditionally, the wedding thank-you note is formal and handwritten in black or blue ink, and it should be sent within three months of the ceremony.
- The recommended formal stationery is of good quality and ecru or white in color with a matching envelope. Pastel colors have also become acceptable. Consider ordering your thank-you notes when you order your wedding invitations.
- The traditional wedding fold-over, or "informal," note is approximately $5\frac{1}{4}$" × $3\frac{1}{2}$" and is typically personalized with your name or monogram. Order or purchase your stationery in advance so you're ready to go when you return from your honeymoon.
- Compose a draft on the computer of what you want to say *before* handwriting the actual note. Because brides and grooms have so many notes to write, you can use the same note and personalize it for each individual.
- You'll be writing a lot of notes, so there is a tendency to become repetitive, which can make your thank-you sound stale and generic. Refer to "The Thank-You Thesaurus" in Chapter 1 and the sample letters in this chapter to get some fresh ideas. There are many ways to say the same thing, only better!
- To be sure your handwriting follows a straight line, you can slide a lined sheet of paper underneath your note or use a plastic envelope writing template. You can also use a ruler or anything with a straight edge to guide your ink pen. And leave some room on the page—don't jam it all together!
- Before you seal the envelope, read your note *out loud* to make sure you didn't miss a word or two. Always double-check the spelling of the name and address.
- If you have a large wedding with hundreds of guests, consider sending out "gift acknowledgment" cards so people will know that their gifts have been received and that a thank-you note is on the way. This gives you more time to write a proper thank-you note.

- For wedding gifts, never text or send email thank-you notes. If someone took the time to send you a gift, their efforts should be recognized appropriately. Texting is acceptable only to let the gift-giver know you received the gift, but a proper thank-you note must still be sent. Also, remember that with package tracking notifications, the gift-giver will likely know when the gift was delivered.
- Don't use your bad handwriting as an excuse not to send a thank-you! If you must, you can go the computer-generated route. Use a script font like Monotype Corsiva and print your thank-you notes on gorgeous stationery—then sign them personally.
- You may actually receive gifts for up to a year, so remember to send notes for any gifts that arrive after the event itself. It's easy to forget when you've already completed your big batch of thank-you notes.
- If you happen to miss sending a thank-you note within that three-month period or close to it, try to be gracious about the error. Write something like "In all the excitement of the wedding, I somehow managed to separate your gift from your card..." or "Many apologies for the tardiness of my note. As you can imagine, we are still getting used to married life..."

THE VIRTUAL THANK-YOU—STATIONERY WEBSITES AND APPS

If you are embracing technology, there are some wonderful and elegant online stationery options available to help you send your wedded gratitude. Check out these ideas when you want to make it digital:

- **Stationery websites:** There are several stationery and invitation websites that will allow you to create online wedding invitations, with options to upload your images and print and manage thank-yous. Check out TinyPrints.com, Minted.com, and PaperlessPost.com for some options.
- **Stationery apps:** If you choose to use one of the digital stationery apps via a mobile device that will print your thank-you card and send it through the postal mail—do your research and test it first by mailing a sample card to yourself. These apps allow you to upload images of your special day, as well as preload

your recipients in the address book, write your note, and in some apps, personally sign the card. The choices of templates, colors, envelopes, and fonts make it easy to express your gratitude. Tip: If you have a wonderful picture from the wedding; group shot at the shower; the two of you on your honeymoon; or even a selfie with you, the gift-giver, and the gift, add it to your note. Check out Ink on the app store for a good option.

MONOGRAMS

Monograms are always in style and represent a certain sense of tradition and class. They are personal to you and add a bit of elegance to the presentation of your thank-you notes, stationery, or whatever you'd like to put them on. Here are a few examples:

• **First, middle, surname, or maiden name:** Use your first, middle, and last name or maiden name (a woman's surname before marriage) to create your monogram.

First Name + Middle Name + Last Name

If you are using initials that are all the same height, they should follow the order of your name. Your monogram would look like this:

FML

If you are using initials that vary in height, your last name would be in the middle:

*F**L**M*

• **Married woman using maiden and married name:** If using your partner's surname, your maiden name moves into the position of your middle name, and your married surname will take the place of your maiden name or can be hyphenated.

First Name + Maiden Name + Partner Surname OR
First Name + Maiden Name-Partner Surname

If you are using initials of the *same* size, your new monogram would look like this:

FMP

With initials of *different* heights, your new married surname will be in the middle:

$$F\mathbf{P}M$$

- **Same-sex couple retaining surnames:** If you are retaining your surnames; for example:

First Name + Middle Name + Surname

&

First Name + Middle Name + Surname

Your monogram may be written on the same line using your first and surname with a separation. Using the names *Thomas **A**ppleton and Richard **Z**appa,* the monogram would look like this:

TA RZ

Another option is to use the *first initial* of the *first name* on the outside and the *first initial* of the *surnames* on the inside to signify the union. For example:

$$T\mathbf{AZ}R$$

TIPS FOR SOCIAL MEDIA WEDDING AND HASHTAGGING

Weddings are exciting events, and in the joy of experiencing the moment of "I do!" your guests will be the first to record and upload memories on social media sites for all to see. In the spirit of sharing your joy with others, things can sometimes get out of hand. Here are some tips to help keep your wedding magnificently ceremonial:

- **Define your social media rules before your wedding.** Pictures are a welcome gift, but you can politely ask your guests to wait until the ceremony has concluded before they begin posting online. Being present in the sacredness of the ritual they were asked to witness is important.
- **Display your wedding hashtag** so when your guests post images and "tag" you on social media sites, they have a designated hashtag to use and a searchable link so you can see the images and use them in your thank-you notes! When

you create your tag, make sure it is unique to you by perhaps including the year, and then search for the hashtag to ensure no one else has used it (for example, #MrandMrsJonesYEAR).

- **Offer Wi-Fi to your guests.** Print the secure network name on table cards or write it creatively on a chalkboard with your hashtag so your guests can easily upload any images your photographer might miss. Consider taking this opportunity to thank your guests for coming by printing a note like *Our dear family and friends, thank you for being an important part of our lives and joining us today to celebrate our love.* Or *We adore you and hope you have the time of your lives as we begin ours—together.*

- **Use technology by connecting live!** For your remote loved ones around the world who can't attend your sacred vows in person, you can livestream the ceremony via social media sites and videoconferencing platforms. It's also a brilliant way to remotely open your gifts together and stay connected to the people you love and cherish.

THANK GUESTS VIA A CHARITY DONATION

To thank all your cherished guests and/or honor loved ones who have passed away, consider making a donation instead of giving wedding favors and announcing this information on a card. This is a heartfelt way to begin a new life together while making a difference. Make up your own verse or scout the amazing ideas and phrasing shared by hundreds of grateful couples online. Here's an example:

In lieu of favors,
a donation to (name of charity) has been made
in your honor and to celebrate our loved ones
who join us in spirit.
From the bottom of our hearts,
thank you for the blessings you have given us
and for being a treasured part of our lives.

(Name of Bride and Groom)
(Wedding Date)

> **❝I WOULD RATHER SHARE ONE LIFETIME WITH YOU THAN FACE ALL THE AGES OF THIS WORLD ALONE.❞**
>
> —Arwen, Fran Walsh and Peter Jackson,
> *The Lord of The Rings: The Fellowship of the Ring* screenplay

I DO, I DO, AND THANK YOU TOO—SAMPLE NOTES

Here are sample thank-you notes to help you let everybody in your extended wedding party know how much their contributions mean to both of you.

THANK YOU TO THE BRIDE OR GROOM'S PARENT(S) FOR THE WEDDING

Dear _____,

Words cannot describe my sincere appreciation to you (both) for giving (name of spouse) and me the wedding of our dreams. Thank you for every single detail you made possible, for your patience when mine wore thin, the advice you never thought I heard, your unconditional love, and for just being there.

With all my love, always,

_____

CANDLESTICKS

Dear _____,

(Name of spouse) joins me in thanking you for the gorgeous candlesticks. We just love them and have already set them out on our table. We will savor the beautiful ambiance they bring to all our special meals! Thank you so very much.

With love,

_____

CHINA OR DINNERWARE

Dear _____,

We are overwhelmed by your generous gift. You couldn't possibly imagine how many (china/dinnerware) patterns we looked at before we finally picked this one. We will think of you both every time we use our fabulous dishes! Thank you!

Sincerely,

_____

COOKWARE OR COOKBOOK

Dear _____,

We just can't thank you enough for the spectacular (cookware/cookbook)! You know we love to cook, and with all the kitchen items we've received, we're sure to be in fierce competition with world-class chefs. Now we can make all the very best gourmet meals. After we've had a chance to practice a recipe or two, we'd love to have you both over for dinner.

Sincerely yours,

_____

Dear _____,

I really believe the kitchen is the heartbeat of the home—where celebrations are created and cherished recipes shared and enjoyed by our loved ones. Thank you for the gorgeous (cookware) that will allow me to infuse my love into good food and heartfelt memories I know my family will treasure. Thank you for such a lovely and thoughtful gift.

With all my love,

_____

CRYSTAL OR GLASSWARE

Dear _____,

When I met (name of spouse), I felt as though I had experienced the most sparkling thing in the world. That is, until we opened your gift last night! Thank you for the (crystal/glasses)—they are just magnificent. We were so excited that we opened a very special bottle of champagne and toasted you for your love and thoughtfulness! Cheers!

Love,

_____

FILL-IN-THE-BLANKS—GENERAL GIFT

Dear _____,

The one thing we desperately needed was (name of gift). You would not believe how many times we have already used it this week alone. Thank you so much—we just love it! More important, thank you from the bottom of our hearts for sharing this special day with us. It would not have been the same without you!

Sincerely,

_____

Dear _____,

I know I thanked you at the reception, but I want to let you both know how much we appreciate the lovely (name of gift) you gave us. We hope you had a wonderful time at our wedding...it meant so much to us that you were there to help celebrate our new life together. Thank you!

With affection,

_____

FRAME

Dear _____,

Thank you so much for the beautiful frame! We really wanted a special one for our wedding picture, and this one is just stunning. Please know that when we look at it, we will think of your generosity. We hope you had a wonderful time at the wedding and thank you for joining us.

Most sincerely,

_____

FOOD PROCESSOR, STAND MIXER, OR BLENDER

Dear _____,

We were really hoping we would get the (food processor/stand mixer/ blender)! You have single-handedly cut our kitchen time in half and helped us create delicious (meals/smoothies). We can't wait to have you over to celebrate love, great food, and your wonderful friendship! Hope you had as terrific a time at the wedding as we did! Our most sincere thanks!

Love,

_____

GIFT CERTIFICATES AND GIFT CARDS

Dear _____,

You can't imagine our excitement when we opened your present! Thank you so much for your very generous gift card. Now we can go on a shopping spree and get everything we need to set up our home together. We are just thrilled! From the bottom of our hearts, thank you.

Gratefully yours,

_____

HONEYMOON GIFT CARD—HOTEL, AIRLINE, OR TRAVEL

Dear _____,

Oh, thank you so very much! Your presence at our wedding was a gift in itself, but the gift card to the (name of hotel/airline/travel company) for our honeymoon was simply spectacular. We so appreciate your generosity. Thank you for giving us the gift of a memory together that we will cherish for a lifetime.

With our love and thanks,

_____

MONEY

Dear _____,

Thank you very much for the incredibly generous (check/gift of cash) you gave us! It was so thoughtful of you and we appreciated your beautiful card and note of best wishes. Please know that we are saving up to buy a (home/car/miscellaneous) and your gift gives us a wonderful start. Thank you so much for your generosity, continued love, and being an important part of our special day.

With our gratitude,

_____

MONOGRAMMED TOWELS

Dear _____,

What a perfect and lovely gift! Thank you for the gorgeous cotton towels. We desperately needed matching ones and having a set complete with our new monogram feels simply luxurious. We hope you had a wonderful time at our wedding—it meant so much to us to have you there.

With love,

_____

PLATTER OR SERVING DISH

Dear _____,

What a gorgeous (platter/serving dish)! No matter what we serve on it, it's going to look delicious! We love it and look forward to using it at our next festive occasion. Thank you so much for thinking of us and for being such good friends.

Sincerely,

_____

SILVER, SILVER PLATE, OR SILVER PLACE SETTING

Dear _____,

(Name of spouse) and I screamed when we opened your "sterling" gift. We absolutely love the silver (name of item)! We just can't express how grateful we are; (it is/they are) simply lovely. We will definitely enjoy (it/them) on each and every special occasion.

Thank you!

_____

VASE

Dear _____,

You can't imagine how excited we were when we opened your gift. We really wanted a beautiful vase! It is so stunning that we immediately placed it on the mantel over the fireplace. Now we have a really great excuse to keep the living room filled with beautiful flowers. Thank you so much for thinking of us and helping us celebrate our wedding.

With love,

_____

THANK YOU TO THE PERFORMER OF THE CEREMONY

Dear (Reverend/Father/Rabbi/Name),

It is with great joy that I write this note to thank you for performing the wedding ceremony for (name of spouse) and me. We so appreciated the time you took to meet with us and make sure that every element of the ceremony was just right. I know that marriage can be trying at times, but we truly feel that with the tools of honor, communication, and trust you have shared with us, we are sure to be prepared for anything that comes our way. Thank you so very much for blessing our bond to each other.

Respectfully yours,

_____

TO THE PARENT(S) FROM THE BRIDE OR GROOM FOR THE REHEARSAL DINNER

Dear _____,

I want you to know how much I appreciated the rehearsal dinner you gave us—it was magnificent in every way. A special night, surrounded by only our closest of family and friends, filled our hearts with joy and made us feel like the luckiest couple in the whole world. As you rose to toast us, I swelled with emotion, reflecting on every single moment you've given me to create my wonderful life. As I look forward to creating a new chapter, please know it is built on the foundation of the virtues of love and gratitude you have instilled in me.

With my love, always,

_____

Happily Ever After *Anniversary* Gifts

YEAR	TRADITIONAL	MODERN
1	Paper	Clock
2	Cotton	China
3	Leather	Crystal or glass
4	Fruit or flowers	Appliances
5	Wood	Silverware
6	Candy or iron	Wooden objects
7	Wool or copper	Desk sets
8	Bronze	Linens or lace
9	Pottery or willow	Leather goods
10	Tin or aluminum	Diamond jewelry
11	Steel	Fashion jewelry
12	Silk or linen	Pearls or colored gems
13	Lace	Textiles or furs
14	Ivory	Gold jewelry
15	Crystal	Watches
16	Silver	Hollowware
17	Wine or spirits	Furniture
18	Appliances	Porcelain
19	Jade	Bronze

YEAR	TRADITIONAL	MODERN
20	China	Platinum
21	Fire (theme)	Brass or nickel
22	Water (theme)	Copper
23	Air (theme)	Silver plate
24	Stone (theme)	Musical instruments
25	Silver	Sterling silver
26	Art	Original artwork
27	Music	Sculpture
28	Linens	Orchids
29	Tools	New furniture
30	Pearl	Diamond
31	Travel	Timepieces
32	Bronze	Conveyances/automobiles
33	Iron	Amethyst
34	Food	Opal
35	Coral or jade	Jade
40	Ruby	Ruby
45	Sapphire	Sapphire
50	Gold	Gold

WEDDING PARTY THANK-YOUS

Dear _____,

I can't believe this moment has finally arrived. Remember all those times we spent laughing over bad dates—I can't believe I found my person! I want to thank you for always being there for me every single time my heart broke or I cried with joy—you helped bring me to this moment. I treasure our friendship and thank you for standing beside me on my very special wedding day.

Love you,

_____

- -

Dear _____,

We felt so incredibly honored and blessed to have you share this magical moment in our lives. Thank you for being an integral part of our wedding party and sharing your love, laughter, and generous support as we begin this new chapter of our lives.

With our love and gratitude,

_____

CHAPTER 9

Baby SHOWERS, SPIRITUAL CELEBRATIONS, and *First* BIRTHDAYS

THANK YOU, BABY!

> "PIGLET NOTICED THAT EVEN THOUGH HE HAD A VERY SMALL HEART, IT COULD HOLD A RATHER LARGE AMOUNT OF GRATITUDE."
>
> —A.A. Milne, English author, *Winnie-the-Pooh*

Finding out you are expecting a baby is one of the most exciting moments you can experience. In that split second, a tiny heartbeat will change your world forever, and nothing will ever be the same. Whatever your spiritual beliefs, life is a gift we are universally thankful for, and when the miracle of birth has been bestowed upon you, you will never take for granted the blessings you have been given. How you announce your child to the world is also significant. That child's presence will have an impact that reaches beyond your own life, touching the hearts of your family, friends—and perhaps the world.

ONLINE BABY REGISTRIES

The most efficient way to keep track of all your baby gifts is with an online baby registry. Most store registries let you see who purchased registered items, along with their contact information. Some provide a "welcome kit" and "completion discount" to help you get everything on your list. For example, *Amazon*'s baby registry allows you to create and send a digital thank-you note to the gift-giver via their platform; to create "group gift giving" for specific gifts; and to set up a "diaper fund" and easy returns, or request gift cards that can be used for anything on their marketplace. (See Chapter 2's section "Online Gift Registries and Thank-You Lists" for additional tips.)

DOS AND DON'TS FOR BABY SHOWER THANK-YOUS

There is so much to remember when preparing for baby's arrival. Here are some dos and don'ts to keep you organized when you and baby are showered with love:

- Do pick up or order your thank-you note stationery and postage stamps online before your baby shower.
- Do ask someone at your shower to make a list of every gift you receive and write down who gave it.
- Do consider picking up a nice name and address book to pass around so your guests can write down their current contact information.
- Do remember to refer to Chapter 1: Thank-You Notes 101 for your thank-you note guidelines and how to properly address an envelope.
- Don't forget to send a thank-you note to the person who hosted your shower.
- Do handwrite your notes and keep them looking as elegant and gracious as possible.
- Do start writing and sending out your notes as soon as possible after the shower.
- Don't ever use email to send out your baby thank-you notes.
- If you want to go the electronic route and send a digital thank-you, check out some of the stationery apps that will send your note as a postcard or in an envelope through the postal mail.

TEN THINGS EVERY GRATEFUL NEW PARENT SHOULD KNOW ABOUT THANK-YOU NOTES

Always remember the importance of your health and your baby's health. Don't let your thank-you notes stress you out. If you are feeling overwhelmed, write one a day until they are finished. Cherish this time—it passes far too quickly. Here are some tips for writing those thank-you notes while caring for a little one:

1. If you are ordering birth announcements, purchase your thank-you notes at the same time. It's one less thing you'll have to worry about later on.
2. Trying to cut costs? Send paper birth announcements to close friends and family to have as treasured keepsakes and send the balance of your announcements digitally via email or a social media post.
3. Just about everything—from personalized thank-you notes, beautiful postage stamps, return address self-inking stamps, black or blue ink pens, and even what you'll need for the baby—can be ordered online and delivered to your front door.
4. It's a good rule to send out your thank-you notes within two weeks, but if you miss the time frame, add something like, "With the sleepless nights of our precious new baby, all the days have rolled into one..."
5. After the baby is born, it's likely more presents and flowers will arrive. Even though everyone understands that you just had a baby, they still expect a thank-you note.
6. If you receive a gift of flowers, it's always a good idea to call the person who sent them, so you match the same level of enthusiasm with which the flowers were sent. If you aren't up to it, then have your partner contact them on your behalf.
7. If you get flowers delivered to your room in the hospital and you just aren't up to having a conversation with anyone (understandable!), you can take a picture and text it to the gift-giver with a short line of thanks. Make sure you bring the gift enclosure cards home with you so you won't forget to send a note later.
8. Remember to wait before removing the tags on baby clothes and keep gift receipts until after the baby is born in case you need to make exchanges. If you can't return or exchange the gifts, consider donating the items to a charity that can give them to parents who really need them.

9. Keep the gift enclosure cards and note the item on the back of each. Mark it with a check or star when you've sent your thank-you note and put the gift cards in your baby box.
10. Make sure to thank all the people in your life who supported you through your pregnancy—and put up with you during your mood swings and cravings too. If you're adopting, thank all the people who helped bring that little miracle into your arms!

BABY SHOWER THANK-YOUS—SAMPLE NOTES

When you're getting ready to welcome a new addition to the family, the demands of pregnancy and preparing for a baby can make it difficult just to keep up with your busy schedule. In addition, there are what seems like hundreds of thank-you notes to write before, during, and after the baby for months to come. Just when you think you've received your last gift and sent off your final thank-you note, you get another present! Still, it's important to let your friends and family know how much you appreciate their love, support, and generosity during this special time. So whether you're expecting or adopting, here are some suggestions and sample thank-yous to help you express your gratitude and still keep your strength.

BABY BOOK OR PHOTO ALBUM

Dear _____,

Your presence at my shower was a gift in itself. Thank you for the gorgeous (baby book/photo album). I am really looking forward to filling the pages and capturing every single moment the baby does anything. Thank you again for all your love and support.

With my love,

_____

> **WHEN THE FIRST BABY LAUGHED FOR THE FIRST TIME, ITS LAUGH BROKE INTO A THOUSAND PIECES, AND THEY ALL WENT SKIPPING ABOUT, AND THAT WAS THE BEGINNING OF FAIRIES.**
>
> —J.M. Barrie, Scottish author, *Peter Pan*

BABY/VIDEO MONITOR

Dear _____,

It was so thoughtful of you to send us a gift for (baby's name). I had no idea I would be so nervous each and every single time I stepped out of the baby's room for fear I wouldn't hear (him/her/them) crying. Having your gift of a baby monitor has given me the freedom to do normal daily things like take a shower! Now my mind is at ease, knowing I will be able to (listen/see) my little one(s) and be there when (he/she/they) need(s) me, no matter where I am in the house (or even at work)! Thank you!

Sincerely yours,

_____

BLANKET

Dear _____,

I absolutely adore the beautiful (satin/cotton/muslin) receiving blanket and am looking forward to using it. I still can't believe that very soon I will have a cute little bundle of joy! Thank you so much for such a lovely and thoughtful gift to snuggle the baby in. I know the baby will love it as much as I do.

With love,

_____

BOOK(S)

Dear _____,

There is nothing more wonderful than the gift of books! Thank you so much for giving (name of child) (name of book) and helping us build such a wonderful library. We are looking forward to reading our little angel to sleep and filling (her/his/their) mind with wonderful stories. Your thoughtfulness is so appreciated.

Thank you,

_____

CAR SEAT

Dear _____,

What a thoughtful gift! Just think, the very first thing the baby will be nestled in as (he/she/they) leave(s) the hospital for a safe journey home is your car seat. Thank you for the one thing I needed most! Even more important, thank you for being with me at my shower. Your presence made the day that much more special to me.

With affection,

_____

CLOTHING

Dear _____,

I just want to thank you again for the beautiful things you gave us for (baby's name). They are all lovely and certainly arrived in the nick of time. (She/He/They) (is/are) already wearing the (name of item), dripping milk all over and quite honestly being the most beautiful baby I could have ever wished for. Thank you so much for thinking of us; we really appreciate it. Please send our love to (name of spouse/partner/relative).

Love,

_____

FILL-IN-THE-BLANKS—BABY

Dear _____,

What an incredible surprise it was to open the front door this afternoon and find a big box addressed to the baby. I love the (name of item)! That was definitely one thing I absolutely needed to have for our little one. Thank you for such a thoughtful gift for our sweet pea.

With love,

_____

MONEY, STOCK, SAVINGS BONDS—COLLEGE FUND

Dear _____,

Thank you so much for the generous (financial gift) you gave us for the baby. We have decided to (put it in/open up) the baby's (savings account/ college fund). Please know it will be put to good use to secure a good foundation for (his/her/their) future. Thank you for your thoughtfulness and for giving our little one just what (he/she/they) needed.

With much love,

_____

> **THE MOST BEAUTIFUL THINGS IN THE WORLD CANNOT BE SEEN OR TOUCHED, THEY ARE FELT WITH THE HEART.**
>
> —Antoine de Saint-Exupéry, French author, *The Little Prince*

STROLLER

Dear _____,

Oh, you shouldn't have, but we are so thankful you did! We love the (brand name) stroller for the baby. It will take us from the baby stages all the way past the toddler years and then some! Now we will be able to stroll (down the avenue/through the mall) and shop while our little one relaxes in total luxury. Thank you so much! We love it!

With affection,

_____

SHOWER HOST/HOSTESS—FROM THE MOMMY OR DADDY-TO-BE

Dear _____,

Words cannot express how much I appreciate your giving me a baby shower! It was truly the best party I have ever been to, and I had such an amazing time being with everyone. From the tiny party favors to the delicious cupcakes and all the fun games—everything was simply perfect. Thank you for making me feel so wonderful. I am blessed to have you in my life.

Love,

_____

SHOWER HOST/HOSTESS—FROM A GRATEFUL GUEST

Dear _____,

I want to thank you for including me in your beautiful celebration for (name of parent-to-be) and their forthcoming bundle of joy! I know I speak for everyone in saying that we all had a wonderful time, playing games, enjoying all the delicious treats, and enjoyed spending time in your lovely home. You are truly a gracious (host/hostess), and it was a pleasure to be part of the festivities. Thank you so very much.

Sincerely yours,

_____

CHRISTENING OR BRIS—SAMPLE NOTES

FILL-IN-THE-BLANKS

Dear _____,

What an honor it was to have you celebrate (baby's name) (christening/ bris) with us. We were simply thrilled when we opened your thoughtful and generous gift. Please know the (name of gift) is something that we are certain the baby will cherish for a lifetime. Thank you for your kindness and blessings.

Love,

_____

Dear _____,

Thank you so very much for joining my family to celebrate my special day. I simply adore the (name of gift) you gave me, and I will think of you every time I (see it/use it). More important, I so appreciate all of the love and support you have given to my family. From my little heart, I thank you. May God bless you and your family.

Wishing you love and peace,

_____

Dear _____,

On behalf of our family, thank you for blessing our child with your love and best wishes. We so deeply appreciated your presence, the thoughtful gifts you gave us, and being a part of this special tradition in all our lives. May God bless you always.

Respectfully yours,

_____

OFFICIATING PRIEST, REVEREND, FATHER

Dear _____,

You are indeed a very special and inspiring person to us. We want you to know that you have affected not only our lives but also the lives of the families in our community. We are so grateful to you for the service you have given in God's name. We humbly thank you for initiating our child into God's divine grace through baptism and welcoming (her/him/them) into the church.

Yours faithfully,

_____

THANK YOU TO BABY'S GRANDPARENT(S) FOR THEIR ADVICE

Dear _____,

I just want to thank you for all the help and advice you have given me with the baby. Knowing you are there to lend a shoulder to cry on and answer my call for help in the middle of the night when the baby is crying...well, screaming...has been a godsend for me. I only hope I am as wonderful a parent as you have been to me. I love you and thank you always.

Love,

_____

P.S. When can you babysit?

Easy Etiquette

Traditionally, when sending notes, letters, or general correspondence to a member of the clergy, you would use a closing such as "Respectfully yours" or "Faithfully yours."

FIRST BIRTHDAYS—SAMPLE NOTES

Baby's first birthday is always an exciting event as we look back on the first year of this incredible little life and know we will cherish those moments forever. It's a good idea to pass along the gift of gratitude to your children and teach them how to send their own thank-you notes once they're able to write. In the meantime, here you'll find a few thank-you notes from baby that you can copy, modify, or use as inspiration to write them from yourself to help you focus on the real blessings in your life—your baby!

ARTS AND CRAFTS

Dear _____,

It was so wonderful to see you at my birthday party. I really enjoyed opening your present and discovering the (arts and crafts item) you gave me! As a matter of fact, I am already making fabulous things, and my (mother/father/parent) is delighted I am working on my creativity—as long as I'm outside. Thank you for such an imaginative gift!

With affection,

_____

FILL-IN-THE-BLANKS

Dear _____,

I just want to thank you for coming to my birthday party. It was so wonderful to have you there to celebrate with me. I love the (name of gift) you gave me. It is the perfect thing for me to play with! Thank you for your thoughtfulness.

Sincerely,

_____

Dear _____,

Thank you for celebrating my first birthday with me. I really appreciate the (name of gift) you gave me too. It was the one thing I wanted, and I look forward to playing with it every day! I appreciate your generosity. Please let my parents know when we can set up a playdate!

Your friend,

_____

Dear _____,

You can't imagine my excitement when I opened your gift! I love the (name of gift) and am already enjoying playing with it. Thank you so much for your generosity and for thinking of me on my birthday.

Love,

_____

GIFT CARDS

Dear _____,

What a pleasure it was to have you celebrate my birthday with me. I loved the gift cards you gave me too! I look forward to going shopping and picking out all my favorite things. Thank you for a very special gift.

With affection,

_____

STUFFED ANIMAL

Dear _____,

I could barely contain myself as I ripped the tissue off your present to find out what was inside. I was so excited when I saw a little (color of bear/ other animal) ear sticking out—I just knew I had a new best friend! I want you to know that ("Teddy"/name of stuffed animal) and I are crazy about each other. Oops, have to go—he's in the kitchen looking for (the honey/ food)! Thank you!

Love + honey,
_____ XO

CHAPTER 10

It's the *Holidays!*

CELEBRATING THE SEASON OF GIVING

> AND THE GRINCH, WITH HIS GRINCH-FEET ICE COLD IN THE SNOW,
> STOOD PUZZLING AND PUZZLING, HOW COULD IT BE SO? 'IT CAME WITHOUT
> RIBBONS. IT CAME WITHOUT TAGS. IT CAME WITHOUT PACKAGES, BOXES
> OR BAGS.' AND HE PUZZLED AND PUZZLED TILL HIS PUZZLER WAS SORE.
> THEN THE GRINCH THOUGHT OF SOMETHING HE HADN'T BEFORE. 'WHAT
> IF CHRISTMAS,' HE THOUGHT, 'DOESN'T COME FROM A STORE. WHAT IF
> CHRISTMAS, PERHAPS, MEANS A LITTLE BIT MORE.'

—Dr. Seuss, American author, *How the Grinch Stole Christmas!*

The contagious spirit of the holiday season is filled with the cherished traditions we celebrate with our dear ones, which include love and forgiveness, sharing our laughter and tears, giving and receiving gifts, nostalgic music, and holiday food. We are grateful for the simple things, like a plentiful harvest, the gift of light, the miracle of birth, and, after the cold winter—the new blessings of spring. It is no wonder that cultures around the world embrace the celebrations of the fall and winter seasons with traditions dating back thousands of years.

Every opportunity you have to celebrate something, no matter how small, should always be taken. Let this holiday season be a constant reminder that this special time of year is what *you* make of it. In this chapter, you will learn the power of the holiday card, as well as creating the festive spirit of appreciation. Included are sample holiday thank-you notes to help you express your gratitude. May the blessings of the season be with you the whole year through.

THE POWER OF THE HOLIDAY CARD

Holiday cards create an opportunity to reconnect with loved ones and perhaps even forgive past hurt feelings, letting bygones be bygones, or raising the possibility of renewing a past relationship. Turn up the holiday tunes, sip hot cocoa, and have fun with this classic holiday tradition dating back to the 1800s. Here are some ways to communicate over the holiday season:

- **Write a holiday thank-you note**—Your holiday gift need not be wrapped up in ribbons and bows—it could simply be a thoughtful note of gratitude written inside a holiday card expressing your appreciation to someone who has made a difference in your life.

- **Share an update on your life**—What's happening in your life is always great news to share, but be sure to include all the people and things you are grateful for and that enrich your wonderful life.

- **Foster peace**—Want to make amends? Let goodwill begin with you so you know you did the best you could. *I'm sorry. I ask forgiveness. I forgive you. I wish you love and happiness—always.* If you have apologized and that person continues to hold a grudge, so be it—at least you know you offered a sign of peace. Now release it.

- **Mail a family recipe**—Do you remember that secret family recipe? Capture traditions by writing down your favorite family recipe and include it in your holiday card for your family and friends to enjoy. If you have one, include a picture from the past featuring that famous dish or maybe the person who inspired it.

- **Send cards with photos**—You can easily upload your images to your favorite online stationery websites or apps. With dozens of options to choose from, cards can be sent out for you or sent to your address to mail yourself. Do check out TinyPrints.com, Minted.com, Crane.com, Hallmark.com, and AmericanGreetings.com, as well as apps like Ink for your mobile device.

- **Include tea or hot cocoa with your card**—Slipping a bag of your favorite foil-wrapped holiday tea or hot chocolate into your greeting card is always a good idea! Tip: Set a virtual date on a digital platform for a holiday tea party with loved ones who live far away—it's a warm and sweet way to connect, no matter how far the distance that separates you.

- **Thank employees and customers**—If you own a business, the holidays are a good time to share your gratitude. Customers want to know you appreciate their business and the people who work for you want to feel recognized for their hard work. Thank everyone—there's enough paper to go around to acknowledge every single person with a card and make them feel they are important—because they are. Tell them "I appreciate you! Thank you!"
- **Make a donation to charity**—In lieu of a gift, make a holiday donation for your business as well as for friends and family. In your card, write something such as "Celebrating the spirit of goodwill, a donation has been made in your name to (name of charity)."
- **Don't forget other holidays!**—Send a "thank you for the magic of your spirit" card for Halloween, a "love you to the moon" card for Valentine's Day, a "thanks+giving" card to everyone in your spirit circle, or a "just because" card at any time of the year. Thoughtful cards are always meaningful and bring a wonderful, unexpected burst of surprise when the recipient receives it—because you thought of them.

Easy Etiquette

Set a reminder for the Tuesday after Thanksgiving and be a part of the global movement #GivingTuesday, which has inspired "hundreds of millions of people to give, collaborate, and celebrate generosity." For details, visit www.givingtuesday.org.

> ❝ ALL YOU CAN TAKE WITH YOU IS THAT WHICH YOU'VE GIVEN AWAY. ❞
> — George Bailey, Frank Capra, *It's a Wonderful Life* screenplay

CREATING THE FESTIVE SPIRIT

Spread the spirit of the holiday season by showing your love and appreciation to your family and friends near or far.

- **Thanksgiving and Friendsgiving** are wonderful opportunities to celebrate with your loved ones and to give thanks for their year-round care and support. When you are hosting a gathering, ask each guest to express three things they are grateful for, or create a "Thanks+Giving Fill-in-the-Blanks" list of what they are thankful for in their lives. Tip: Ask everyone to bring their favorite dish! Eat, drink, and be merry!

- **Holiday movies** are a good idea any time of the year. They bring us right into the lives of the people who live in that enchanted, wintry, small country town who learn to appreciate what really matters. It's that little bit of magic that touches our hearts and makes us believe that dreams really do come true.

- **Sweet treats like cakes, cookies, and candy** are always a great way to express your gratitude. Either homemade or store-bought, create your signature holiday gift for you to remember the people you care about in a most delectable way.

- **Making a donation is always a great gift.** Whether you donate your time, your money, your knowledge, or your encouragement, giving is a remarkable gift that you share with someone, making a difference in their life, which makes the world a better place. Every single donation counts...even the pennies on your dresser you don't know what to do with. Tip: Update your AmazonSmile settings so that a portion of your purchases are donated to your favorite charity.

- **Gather long-distance friends and relatives online.** Can't make it home for the holidays? Set up a holiday party via a digital meeting platform. For business or pleasure, for all your holiday celebrations, this is a magical way to express your feelings the entire year. Decorate your virtual background, put on that dashing sweater, and pop the champagne! Don't forget to hit "record" or screenshot the party to preserve your digital memories.

Holiday Phrases

Blessings of the season
Celebrate the season
Deck the Halls
Ho Ho Ho
Jingle all the way...
Love and joy to you.
May all your Christmases be white.
May the festival of lights bring blessings upon you and
all your loved ones.
May the spirit of Christmas be with you always.
May your days be merry and bright.
Peace on earth.
Santa's on his way...
Sending you love + light this holiday and always.
Warmest wishes to you and yours this holiday season.
Wishing you yuletide cheer.

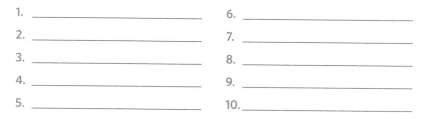

Easy Etiquette

Debra Lassiter and April McLean, founders of Perfectly Polished: The Etiquette School, are the expert teachers of cultivating an attitude of gratitude. They encourage young people to "be confident in who they are to survive the impact of social media. Creating an awareness of gratitude with appreciation of one's self-worth impacts their ability to focus on the positives. Acknowledging, writing, or vocalizing the words *thank you* brings discovery of mindfulness which in turn leads to happier and healthier lives." For more information, visit www.perfectlypolished.com.

WRITE A BLESSINGS LIST—I AM BLESSED BECAUSE…

Writing thank-you notes isn't the only way to show your gratitude. You can also show it to yourself by making a list or keeping a journal of all the things you are grateful for and include what you love about yourself too. Embrace your accomplishments so you can empower yourself! Even better, invite the whole family to do this exercise. The next time you all give or receive, be mindful—feel the magic of gratitude as it fills you up…that spark is contagious—pass it on.

Close your eyes and think about all the blessings in your life, especially on Thanksgiving and as you head into the New Year. Write them down. Begin and end each day with remembering all the wonderful things that are yours.

1. _____
2. _____
3. _____
4. _____
5. _____

6. _____
7. _____
8. _____
9. _____
10. _____

> 66 AS MANY OF YOU KNOW, THE SEASON OF CHANUKAH COMMEMORATES THE VICTORY OF RELIGIOUS FREEDOM....THIS SEASON, RELIGIOUS SEASON, COMMEMORATES THE PERPETUATION OF AGE-OLD DREAMS AND THE HUNGER OF MEN AND WOMEN DOWN THROUGH THE AGES TO MAINTAIN A SPIRIT COMMITTED TO LIFE UNDER THE MOST DIFFICULT CIRCUMSTANCES, THE MOST DIFFICULT PERSECUTIONS, THE MOST DIFFICULT DANGERS, AND UNDER THE MOST DIFFICULT SUFFERING. IT ALSO COMMEMORATES HUMANKIND'S COMMITMENT TO BE FREE. 99
>
> —Chanukah remarks by American president Jimmy Carter at the Lighting of the National Menorah, December 1979

THANK-YOU NOTE DAY—DECEMBER 26

Thank-You Note Day is the perfect opportunity to write your thank-you notes for the gifts you received and remember all the things you are grateful for. The actual day might be different for you depending on what you celebrate, but the spirit is the same. Heat up the leftovers, enjoy the decorations, and start writing! Here are some ways to make the task enjoyable and easy:

- **Refer to Chapter 1 for the basic guidelines on writing your notes and envelopes:** Holiday thank-you notes are not considered formal correspondence, so you can be as creative as you wish. Go ahead and embrace the colors of the season with pen and paper and use your freedom of expression!
- **Assemble a thank-you note box:** Create a box that contains notecards, pens, postage stamps, or stickers. Having everything ready in one place will not only keep you organized but will also help the whole family get it done! Tip: If a child can't write a note, drawing or coloring a picture is a perfect idea and will certainly be appreciated. Refer to my book *101 Ways to Say Thank You! For Kids & Teens* (Cedar Fort Inc., 2015) for more inspiration for young adults all year round.

- **Approach digital thank-yous with the same care as written ones:** The "golden rule" is to always send a handwritten note—it makes an impact and shows your sincere appreciation to the person who took the time to give you a gift. If you must make it digital, definitely try to upload an image of yourself with the gift or even create a video that can be emailed or texted—this is especially nice for our seniors to receive.

SAMPLE HOLIDAY THANK-YOU NOTES

Take some inspiration from these simple fill-in-the-blank ideas—remember, saying thank you is most important!

HOLIDAY GIFT CARD—FILL-IN-THE-BLANKS

Dear _____,

It fits perfectly! Thank you so much for the generous gift card to (name of store). I am so excited to go shopping this week and finally buy (name of item). Thank you for thinking of me and always being so kind! Thank you and Happy Holidays!

Ho Ho Ho,

_____

. . . .

Dear _____,

Thank you for the gift card to (name of store)! It's truly the perfect gift for me, and I can pick out exactly what I want. Thank you for your generosity and for always finding me the most amazing (name of holiday) presents! Happy everything!

Peace,

_____

HOLIDAY GIFT—FILL-IN-THE-BLANKS

Dear _____,

How did you know exactly what I wanted for (name of holiday)! I have been wanting the (name of gift) so much you don't even know! I really appreciate your thoughtfulness. Wishing you a Happy New Year!

Love,

_____

HOLIDAY GIFT—FILL-IN-THE-BLANKS—PHOTO

Dear _____,

Oh my gosh! You give the best presents—always! I love the (name of gift) you sent me. I literally can't wait to (use it/open it/wear it/play with it). I hope you had a wonderful holiday! Wishing you the (merriest of Christmases/happiest Hanukkah/other wish) and a healthy New Year!

Sending you peace + joy,

_____

P.S.—I hope you love this picture!

Dear _____,

Words could not express my excitement when I opened your (name of holiday) gift! You really shouldn't have—but I am so glad you did! Thank you for bringing joy to my world! I just love it! Merry everything! (photo)

Thank you,

_____

HOLIDAY GIFT—DIGITAL DEVICE, GAME, OR TOY

Dear _____,

You know, your gift was the first I reached for! As I tore off the ribbons and paper, I literally screamed and I am sure half the neighborhood could hear my joy! I never thought I would actually get a (name of device or toy). Thank you so so much!! I love it!

Happy (Name of Holiday)!
_____XO

HOLIDAY GIFT—DIGITAL DEVICE

Dear _____,

I truly have no words...I cannot believe it! As I opened your package I was so excited to see what it was! I really needed a new (name of computer/digital device), so this is an amazing gift for me that I will be using every single day. Thank you from the bottom of my heart.

Gratefully yours,

_____

P.S.—I can't wait to (text/email/call) you!!!

> ❝THE YEAR THAT IS DRAWING TOWARDS ITS CLOSE HAS BEEN FILLED WITH THE BLESSINGS OF FRUITFUL FIELDS AND HEALTHFUL SKIES. I DO THEREFORE INVITE MY FELLOW CITIZENS IN EVERY PART OF THE UNITED STATES, AND ALSO THOSE WHO ARE AT SEA AND THOSE WHO ARE SOJOURNING IN FOREIGN LANDS, TO SET APART AND OBSERVE THE LAST THURSDAY OF NOVEMBER NEXT, AS A DAY OF THANKSGIVING.❞

—Proclamation of Thanksgiving by American president Abraham Lincoln, October 1863

HOLIDAY PARTY—THANK YOU!

Dear _____ ,

I woke up this morning still dreaming about your amazing party! I had the most wonderful time and truly did not want to leave. As I rolled into bed, it was safe to say that I realized I had indulged in far too much of all of your delicious treats. Thank you for creating a holiday memory that I will forever cherish! I wish you the happiest of holidays, with good health in the New Year and always!

Love + Light,

_____

Easy Etiquette

You should never go to someone's home for a party or a meal without bringing something. As my mother would say, "Never go empty-handed!" People always appreciate a small token of your appreciation for having you in their home: From a bottle of wine to dessert, a good book, or a great bottle of olive oil—there are many festive things you can bring.

66 SEEING IS BELIEVING, BUT SOMETIMES THE MOST REAL THINGS IN THE WORLD ARE THE THINGS WE CAN'T SEE. 99

—Chris Van Allsburg, American illustrator and author, *The Polar Express*

66 TODAY BEGINS A WEEK-LONG CELEBRATION OF AFRICAN-AMERICAN HERITAGE AND CULTURE THROUGH FAMILY AND COMMUNITY FESTIVITIES. KWANZAA'S SEVEN PRINCIPLES—UNITY, SELF-DETERMINATION, COLLECTIVE WORK AND RESPONSIBILITY, COOPERATIVE ECONOMICS, PURPOSE, CREATIVITY, AND FAITH—ARE ALSO SHARED VALUES THAT BIND US AS AMERICANS...AND COMMIT TO BUILDING A BRIGHTER FUTURE FOR ALL OUR CHILDREN. AS FAMILIES, FRIENDS, AND NEIGHBORS COME TOGETHER TODAY TO LIGHT THE KINARA, OUR FAMILY SENDS OUR BEST WISHES FOR A HAPPY AND HEALTHY NEW YEAR. 99

—Statement by American president Barack Obama on Kwanzaa, December 2015

HOLIDAY DONATION—THANK YOU!

Dear _____,

What we thought was impossible was actually made possible by your generous charitable donation of (money/books/food/clothing) to our (school/foundation/organization). Your gift has allowed us to enrich the lives of our local community, as well as to reach out to those around the world. It only takes one spark to create a fire, and by your continued support you have lit up our ability to raise awareness for (name of cause/a cure). We are forever grateful to you for helping us change the world.

Sincerely yours,

_____

> CHRISTMAS IS A STATE OF MIND. IT IS FOUND THROUGHOUT THE YEAR WHENEVER FAITH OVERCOMES DOUBT, HOPE CONQUERS DESPAIR, AND LOVE TRIUMPHS OVER HATE. IT IS PRESENT WHEN MEN OF ANY CREED BRING LOVE AND UNDERSTANDING TO THE HEARTS OF THEIR FELLOW MAN. THE FEELING IS SEEN IN THE WONDROUS FACES OF CHILDREN AND IN THE HOPEFUL EYES OF THE AGED. IT OVERFLOWS THE HEARTS OF CHEERFUL GIVERS AND THE SOULS OF THE CARING. AND IT IS REFLECTED IN THE BRILLIANT COLORS, JOYFUL SOUNDS, AND BEAUTY OF THE WINTER SEASON. LET US RESOLVE TO HONOR THIS SPIRIT OF CHRISTMAS AND STRIVE TO KEEP IT THROUGHOUT THE YEAR. NANCY AND I ASK YOU TO JOIN US IN A PRAYER THAT PRUDENCE, WISDOM, AND UNDERSTANDING MIGHT DESCEND ON THE PEOPLE OF ALL NATIONS SO THAT DURING THE YEAR AHEAD WE MAY REALIZE AN ANCIENT AND WONDROUS DREAM: 'PEACE ON EARTH, GOODWILL TOWARD MEN.'
>
> —Statement by American president Ronald Reagan on Christmas, December 1981

NEW YEAR'S—CREATING RESOLUTIONS OF SELF-CARE

Making a list of our New Year's resolutions for the coming year is a powerful opportunity to manifest change by taking action in our lives. Remember, if *you* don't invest in your own self-care by taking care of your body, mind, and spirit, *no one will do it for you*. Begin by writing down all the things you are grateful for, what you want in your life, and who you want to stand by your side. Aristotle once said, "We are what we repeatedly do." Create healthy habits with a self-care routine that's all about you, putting yourself and your needs first. If someone is pulling on your time and creating distractions in your life—just say, "No, I must put myself first."

CHAPTER 11

Gestures of APPRECIATION and BELATED Thanks

IT'S NEVER TOO LATE TO SAY THANK YOU

> AT TIMES OUR OWN LIGHT GOES OUT AND IS REKINDLED BY A SPARK
> FROM ANOTHER PERSON. EACH OF US HAS CAUSE TO THINK WITH DEEP
> GRATITUDE OF THOSE WHO HAVE LIGHTED THE FLAME WITHIN US.
>
> —Albert Schweitzer, Nobel laureate

Even the most gracious among us can get so wrapped up in the swirl of life that we put off sending thank-you notes. As the weeks rush by, we find ourselves worrying about our tardiness and wondering how we can ever say thank you now that so much time has passed. There are also those occasions when we realize how influential the kindness of a mentor really was or when the deep loyalty of a friend became essential. We wish we could turn back the clock so we could properly thank that person for making a difference in our lives. The good news is—it's never too late to say thank you. In this chapter, you will find the inspiration you need to reach back and thank the people that gave you a gift and touched your life—from old friends and inspiring people to our essential workers and healthcare heroes.

WRITING A THANK-YOU NOTE FOR SOMETHING THAT HAPPENED A LONG TIME AGO

The format of your thank-you note, even if it is belated, should match the formality of the event or spirit in which the gift, favor, or kindness was given. Handwritten notes are always preferred but what is essential here is conveying to that person or the team of people how important their thoughtfulness was to you. So take a minute, sit down, and write that thank-you!

> 66 SILENT GRATITUDE ISN'T MUCH USE TO ANYONE. 99
>
> —Gladys Bronwyn Stern, English author

Eleven Good Reasons Why It's Never Too Late to Say Thank You

1. Because it's never too late to thank someone for making a difference in your life.
2. Because it's the right thing to do!
3. Because everyone wants to feel appreciated.
4. Because even late thank-yous are powerful, especially when the gift-giver thinks the gift or gesture is forgotten.
5. Because sometimes people have no idea how meaningful their life's contributions have been to you until you tell them.
6. Because the gift of gratitude has the ability to affect people's lives, no matter how late!
7. Because not saying thank you can damage your relationship and reputation.
8. Because the person not thanked may stop giving to you because they feel you didn't appreciate their kindness.
9. Because people will remember the kind of person you were long after you're gone.
10. Because a late thank-you is better than none at all.
11. Do refer to Chapter 1: Thank-You Notes 101 while writing your thank-yous!

IT'S NEVER TOO LATE TO SAY THANK YOU—SAMPLE NOTES

Here you will find thank-you notes that will help you recapture the moment and let the people in your past know you are grateful for their generosity.

THANK YOU FOR BEING MY MENTOR OR IMPORTANT INFLUENCE

Dear _____,

There are no words to express how grateful I am to you for being (my mentor/an important influence). Thank you for sharing with me your life and your hard-earned wisdom. I am so tremendously appreciative. I only hope that one day I can repay the honor.

Sincerely,

_____

....

Dear _____,

For years, I have admired your work not only as a talented businessperson but also as a gracious philanthropist in our community. Through your tireless dedication, you have shown me how essential it is in life to love what you do and never, ever settle for less than what you deserve. Thank you for lighting my way.

Gratefully yours,

_____

THANK YOU, OLD FRIEND

Dear _____,

So many times I think of you and the time we spent together. I wish we could walk back in time, even if only for a moment, and be (age) again. Thank you for being my friend during the good, bad, and in-between. Please know that no matter where life takes us, I will never forget how wonderful you were to me. I wish you love and happiness.

Gratefully yours,

_____

THANK YOU, FRIEND—PHOTO FROM A LIFETIME AGO

Dear _____,

I was cleaning out my boxes and organizing my things when I came across this photo of us. The memories of this moment and the wonderful times we shared came rushing back to me. Do you remember when (memory)?! My goodness, it's like a lifetime ago. You made a difference all those years ago—I will keep these memories sacred in my heart. Enjoy the picture!

Yours truly,

_____

THANK YOU FOR MAKING A DIFFERENCE IN MY LIFE

Dear _____,

There are times in our lives when we are utterly unaware of the effect we have on someone else. I don't know what I would have done without you. There are simply no words to express how grateful I am to you for your kindness, loyalty, love, and selflessness. You have a lifelong friend in me.

With my sincere thanks,

_____

Dear _____,

There is no way I could go back in time and thank you for everything. But I have this moment. I humbly thank you, from the bottom of my heart to the heavens above, for making a difference in my life so many years ago. I am forever grateful.

Yours truly,

_____

THANK YOU, TEACHER

Dear _____,

What a wonderful year we have had together! I wanted to take a moment to thank you for your dedication throughout the year. I know firsthand how hard you worked to finish each special project for the children, and their eyes glowed with such excitement every time you created something wonderful for them. Please know you have left an indelible mark on their memories that they will treasure for a lifetime. Thank you a million times!

With sincere appreciation,

_____

. . . .

Dear _____,

This "Bag of a Million Thank-Yous" is filled with thank-you notes from the faculty, children, and their parents, all of whom were quite taken with the love, creativity, and tireless dedication you gave to your class and our school. Thank you for giving our precious children memories that will last a lifetime. We salute and applaud your tireless efforts.

Sincerely yours,

_____

THANK YOU, DAD AND FATHER FIGURES

Dear Dad,

You are the kind of father every child dreams of having. Beyond compare, you are the kind of man by which others are measured. You are intelligent, accomplished, creative, and handsome—I am so blessed to call you my father. Thank you for always being there and loving me. I adore you.

With all my love,

_____

THANK YOU, MOM AND MOTHER FIGURES

Dear Mom,

Thank you for making me do the things I didn't want to do because they were good for me. Thank you for having the wisdom and patience to let me make mistakes I could learn from. Thank you for encouraging me to finish school when I wanted to see the world. Thank you for holding me through every broken heart. Thank you for making me the person I am today. Thank you for being my mother. I love you so very much.

Love,

_____

> **WE LEARNED ABOUT GRATITUDE AND HUMILITY—THAT SO MANY PEOPLE HAD A HAND IN OUR SUCCESS, FROM THE TEACHERS WHO INSPIRED US TO THE JANITORS WHO KEPT OUR SCHOOL CLEAN...AND WE WERE TAUGHT TO VALUE EVERYONE'S CONTRIBUTION AND TREAT EVERYONE WITH RESPECT.**
>
> —Michelle Obama, American author and first lady

THANKING THE HEALERS—PUBLIC SAFETY WORKERS AND HEALTHCARE PROVIDERS

During an emergency, we are immediately reminded of how precious our life really is and are utterly grateful to the firefighters, police officers, and medical support teams for their selfless intervention. The healers in our world are the real superheroes who sacrifice their own lives in times of crisis to save us. They make our world a better place. We should always take a moment to thank them for all they do for us. If you can't thank them in person, here are a few ideas:

- Write a note of thanks to the medical provider or the team that supported you or your loved one through a crisis—no matter how long ago. It will touch their heart.
- Post a positive thank-you review for the doctor, healthcare staff, or medical facility on a public review or medical review website. It will be an appreciated and visible vote of support and acknowledgment.
- Drop off or arrange for snacks or meals to be delivered with a note of appreciation. It will nurture them as they aid others.
- Ask the facility what they need or donate financially, even in someone's memory. It will keep the grateful goodness going. Tip: Check out AmazonSmile, which donates a percentage of the price of your eligible purchases to your favorite charity.
- Make a personal call of thanks to the fire captain or medical director of the facility and tell them how grateful you are to that firefighter, nurse, doctor, or healthcare provider for their act of kindness. It could change that person's life.

- Post your thank-you shout-out on their social media or your own. It's a great way to keep the blessings coming and share the spirit of generosity. If you are showing your gratitude to your local firefighters for coming to your aid in an emergency or because they have done so much for your community, be sure to tag and/or hashtag your local fire department, the local news station, and/or the individual fire station. Here are some sample notes you can share to thank the public safety workers and healthcare providers that made a difference in your life.

> **IF YOU CAN READ THIS, THANK A TEACHER.**
> —American proverb

THANK YOU, HEALTHCARE HERO

Dear _____,

I wish I kept notes of every single doctor, nurse, and healthcare provider whose love kept my (family member's) spirits up and went above and beyond the call of duty. There were so many supporting us that I would never want any one of them to feel we didn't appreciate every single moment of compassion and strength they gave us. They all did what they had to do and not one person ever complained. Everything they did or we asked for was always done in the very best of spirits. In a short period of time, they became our family. I want to recognize the healthcare team for their extraordinary care and being superheroes when we needed it most. Thank you.

With appreciation,

_____

THANK YOU, DOCTOR OR NURSE

Dear _____,

I just wanted to thank you for being an extraordinary human being. I so appreciated your compassion, integrity, and support during this time of (creating a care plan/treatment/recovery). Thank you for taking the time to speak to us and answer all our questions.

Sincerely yours,

_____

. . . .

Dear _____,

On behalf of our family, I want to thank (medical provider) for being the light of care and compassion we so desperately needed through the crisis of my (loved one/family member's) health. Nothing prepares you for that moment when your loved one's life is in jeopardy. Your mind is racing, spinning, knowing nothing will ever be the same, but you took the time to explain treatment and care options that I couldn't brace myself to face, and you listened to me through my endless tears—thank you for holding me up when I wanted to fall. You touched our lives in a way that will never be forgotten...your passion for patient care is exceptional.

With our deepest gratitude,

_____

> 66 **WHEREVER THE ART OF MEDICINE IS LOVED,
> THERE IS ALSO A LOVE OF HUMANITY.** 99
>
> —Hippocrates, Greek physician

CHAPTER 12

RESPONDING to EXPRESSIONS
of *Symphathy*

FAREWELL, MY FRIEND

> You alone will have stars as no one else has them...
> In one of the stars I shall be living. In one of them I shall be
> laughing. And so it will be as if all the stars will be laughing
> when you look at the sky at night. You, only you, will have stars
> that can laugh! And when your sorrow is comforted (time soothes
> all sorrows) you will be content that you have known me...
> You will always be my friend. You will want to laugh with me.
> And you will sometimes open your window, so, for that pleasure...
> It will be as if, in place of the stars, I had given you a great
> number of little bells that knew how to laugh.

—Antoine de Saint-Exupéry, French author, *The Little Prince*

There comes a time in all our lives when we must say goodbye to a loved one or dear friend. Whether the departure is anticipated or unexpected, it is one of the most heart-wrenching moments we may ever have to endure. Eventually we heal, and over time we are able to laugh again without bursting into tears. Life is a journey, and the extraordinary, truly memorable people we sometimes meet along the way may be there for only a moment, but they linger on in our hearts forever, never to be forgotten.

While we still have the opportunity, it is important that we acknowledge our profound appreciation to those people so deeply meaningful in our lives. When the time does come to say farewell, we will then feel secure in the knowledge that the person we loved so dearly knew it and understood. When we feel as if we can't go on, it is the support, condolences, and love we receive from our friends and family that help us make it through the day. In this chapter, you will find the words you need to thank everyone for their expressions of sympathy.

WRITING THE SYMPATHY THANK-YOU NOTE

The moment will come when you are ready to write your thank-you notes for the support and sympathy you received following the passing of a loved one. All of the basic rules of writing thank-you notes apply; however, there are no restrictions on sending them by a certain time. It's best to keep formality and elegance in your notes as you honor the departed. Remember, too, that many of the people who are receiving your thank-you notes are also grieving.

Thank-yous should be sent to everyone who helped you get through this exceedingly difficult time—the clergy; the pallbearers; those who sent condolence cards, gifts, food, and flowers; or anyone who made a financial contribution or a donation to charity in your loved one's memory.

Ten Sympathetic Sage Tips

1. Do have someone help you if you are unable to write the thank-you notes yourself.
2. Do include the deceased's memorial card in your thank-you note, if you have one. It is a special keepsake for the people who couldn't attend the memorial or funeral. These can be easily ordered through the funeral home or online.
3. Do send a personal, handwritten thank-you for flowers, charity donations, financial contributions, meals, or shoulders you cried on.
4. Do check out the preprinted and personalized sympathy thank-you cards that are available in stationery stores or online.
5. Do write a few words of personal thanks in preprinted sympathy thank-you cards.

6. Don't send emailed sympathy thank-you notes if you can avoid it; they aren't as personal as handwritten notes.
7. Do consider sending sympathy acknowledgment cards if the loved one who passed away was a prominent person and you couldn't possibly send a personal note of thanks to so many people.
8. Do consider publishing a tribute to the deceased in your local newspaper when a public acknowledgment is necessary.
9. Do send a condolence note to a friend who's suffered the loss of a friend or family member. Expressions of sympathy are always appropriate.
10. Do make a post on social media if you wish to thank everyone who sent you their love and prayers electronically.

THANK-YOU ACKNOWLEDGMENTS

If you are interested in printing your own acknowledgment cards, here are some examples of what the phrasing might look like. Remember to include a handwritten personal note of thanks.

The family of
(name of deceased)
acknowledges with deep appreciation your
kind expression of sympathy.
We will forever cherish the life of
(name of deceased)
and eternally wave to the heavens as (he/she)
begins (his/her) journey among the stars.
Our family sincerely thanks you for your
sympathy and thoughtfulness.
(Name of widow/widower/family name)
gratefully acknowledges your loving expression
of sympathy during this sorrowful time of mourning.

> 66 IF ALL THE BEASTS WERE GONE, MEN WOULD DIE FROM A GREAT
> LONELINESS OF SPIRIT, FOR WHATEVER HAPPENS TO THE BEASTS
> ALSO HAPPENS TO THE MAN. ALL THINGS ARE CONNECTED.
> WHATEVER BEFALLS THE EARTH BEFALLS THE SONS OF THE EARTH. 99

—Chief Seattle of the Suquamish Tribe, letter to American president Franklin Pierce

ONLINE CONDOLENCES: USING SOCIAL MEDIA

Social media sites give us a voice to share, grieve, and record memories that connect our hearts. Holding up an electronic candle to the world, we can stand united in a global cause or mourn the passing of a loved one or legendary figure whose life affected us all.

To post or not to post, that is indeed the question when announcing to friends and family that your loved one has passed on to spirit. Here are some tips to help you honor the dearly departed:

- Use social media to ask for positive thoughts, energy, and prayers to be sent to your loved ones and family to help them through this difficult time.
- Before you post a funeral notice on social media, first make sure to contact those people who are most affected by the passing and get their approval.
- If you post an announcement of a celebration of life that is in person or virtual, be sure to include the date, time, location of service, and connection links. Tip: Let everyone know if the family is requesting a charity donation in lieu of flowers.
- Remember, while email is more personal than social media, a personal phone call is still the preferred method to express your condolences.
- Many funeral homes have an "online condolence" website that provides a central place to collect well wishes and share memories of your loved one. The entries people write and share can then be sent to you by email or assembled into a keepsake book.
- Make a post on social media or by email to create a "meal train" to help organize donations of food. Everyone may then feel they are helping the bereaved in some way.

> **GOODBYES ARE ONLY FOR THOSE WHO LOVE WITH THEIR EYES.**
> **BECAUSE FOR THOSE WHO LOVE WITH HEART AND SOUL**
> **THERE IS NO SUCH THING AS SEPARATION.**
>
> —Rumi, Persian poet

Easy Etiquette

The next time you say farewell to someone you love, ask your friends and loved ones to write a note or letter about what that person meant to them. It could be a few words or even a story to share. Keep the notes together or make a treasured memorial book. Long after the flowers have faded and people have returned to their lives, you will cherish these memories for a lifetime, and so will your children.

FOR YOUR KINDNESS AND SYMPATHY—SAMPLE NOTES

Here are a few notes to help you show your friends and family how much you appreciate their love and sympathy.

THANK YOU ON BEHALF OF THE FAMILY

Dear _____,

On behalf of my (family member), please accept (her/his/their) sincere thanks for the (card/letter/flowers/food/financial contribution/other gift) you sent in memory of (name of deceased). It is only the generosity of good friends like you that has gotten us through this very difficult time. Thank you.

Respectfully yours,

_____

THANK YOU FOR YOUR CHARITABLE DONATION

Dear _____,

I know how much (name of deceased) treasured your friendship. If there was anyone in this world (he/she) loved and respected, it was you. Thank you for honoring (him/her) with your generous charitable donation to (name of charity). I am certain (he/she) would be so proud.

With my sincere appreciation,

_____

THANK YOU, CLERGY

Dear _____,

This is definitely a moment in my life when I feel I am being tested by God. It seems so unfair for our loved ones to pass. While I am certain that (name of deceased) is in a better place, it has been so painful to say goodbye with grace and dignity. Thank you for helping me grieve, laugh, and cry. Thank you for showing me how to heal. God bless you.

Faithfully yours,

_____

> MAY THE ROAD RISE TO MEET YOU,
> MAY THE WIND BE ALWAYS AT YOUR BACK.
> MAY THE SUN SHINE WARM UPON YOUR FACE,
> THE RAINS FALL SOFT UPON YOUR FIELDS.
> AND UNTIL WE MEET AGAIN,
> MAY GOD HOLD YOU IN THE PALM OF HIS HAND.
>
> —Irish blessing

THANKS FOR YOUR EXPRESSION OF SYMPATHY

Dear _____,

There are simply no words to thank you for the loving expression of sympathy you have given us during the passing of (name of deceased). We are deeply grateful.

With our love,

_____

THANK YOU FOR THE FLOWERS OR FUNERAL WREATH

Dear _____,

Your love and support during this tremendously difficult time are so greatly appreciated. The gorgeous flowers you sent were spectacular, and I know that (name of deceased) would have loved them. On behalf of my family, I thank you.

Gratefully yours,

_____

> **WHEN YOU COME OUT OF THE STORM, YOU WON'T BE THE SAME PERSON WHO WALKED IN. THAT'S WHAT THIS STORM'S ALL ABOUT.**
>
> —Haruki Murakami, Japanese author

THANK YOU FOR THE FOOD

Dear _____,

I understand you are grieving just as deeply as we are. Please know how much we appreciated the (food item) you brought us. It was absolutely delicious and we know it was made with all of your love. Thank you for taking the time to comfort us.

Sincerely yours,

_____

THANK YOU FOR THE LOVING TRIBUTE

Dear _____,

My (mother/father/other family member/name of deceased) was the light of our life. Thank you for honoring (him/her) with your loving tribute. We are forever grateful for the heartwarming memories you have shared with us, and we will treasure them for a lifetime.

Love,

_____

> **PLEASE WATCH OUT FOR EACH OTHER AND LOVE AND FORGIVE EVERYBODY. IT'S A GOOD LIFE, ENJOY IT.**
>
> —Jim Henson, American puppeteer

CONCLUSION:
CREATE A MINDFUL *Gratitude* SELF-CARE PRACTICE

Embracing the benefits of the magic effect of gratitude in your life must first begin with you. Nothing is more powerful than counting your blessings and being grateful for what you have in this world instead of complaining about the things you don't have. Here are some ideas to make appreciation part of your daily self-care practice:

- **Breathe and meditate:** Every morning before you rise, and in the evening before you go to bed, take a moment to breathe and meditate. Simply close your eyes, put your hands on your chest, and take three deep breaths. Listen to the sound of your life.

- **Addressing envy:** Essentially, jealousy is the absence of gratitude, and it happens to the best of us. Sometimes people we encounter are a "virtual mirror" for whom we would like to be, what we want to have, or what we yearn to attain. When you realize that's what's happening, it's really a self-reflective moment of clarity for you to redirect those feelings to yourself. If you want to inspire change in your life, use this "ah-ha" moment as an opportunity to take a personal action to create what you want.

- **Journal the things you're grateful for:** Create a handwritten journal affirming what *you* are grateful for. Write down three things every day that you are blessed with, things that money can't buy; include the qualities you value most about yourself. Any time you're feeling blue, write one more thing you are grateful for. As you remember with gratitude the food on your table, your family, friends, your health, or the roof over your head, this list can profoundly stabilize your life.

> 66 MAY THE FORCE BE WITH YOU... 99
>
> —George Lucas, American director, Star Wars

INDEX

159